Elements of

Software Science

THE COMPUTER SCIENCE LIBRARY

Operating and Programming Systems Series
Peter J. Denning, *Editor*

OPERATING AND PROGRAMMING SYSTEMS SERIES

Elements of
Software Science

Maurice H. Halstead
Purdue University

NORTH HOLLAND·NEW YORK
NEW YORK • OXFORD

Elsevier North Holland, Inc.
52 Vanderbilt Avenue, New York, New York 10017

Distributors outside the United States and Canada:

Thomond Books
(A Division of Elsevier North Holland Scientific Publishers, Ltd.)
P.O. Box 85
Limerick, Ireland

© 1977 by Elsevier North Holland, Inc.
Third Printing, 1979

Library of Congress Cataloging in Publication Data

Halstead, Maurice Howard, 1918–
    Elements of software science.

    (Operating and programming systems series; 2) (Elsevier computer science library)
    Bibliography: p.
    Includes index.
    I. Computer programs I. Title.
QA76.6.H3   001.6′425   77-1321
ISBN 0-444-00205-7
ISBN 0-444-00215-4 pbk

Manufactured in the United States of America

To Sylvia

Contents

(List of Symbols and Frequently Used Equations appear on page 2)

Preface

This book contains the first systematic summarization of a branch of experimental and theoretical science dealing with the human preparation of computer programs and other types of written material. Application of the classical methods of the natural sciences demonstrates that even such relatively intangible objects as written abstracts and computer programs are governed by natural laws, both in their preparation and in their ultimate form.

The work underlying each chapter of this monograph is firmly based on the methods and principles of classical experimental science. Even so, the results in this area, or more specifically, the concept that significant quantitative results are attainable in such an area, are sufficiently counterintuitive as to appear almost weird.

Intuition, however, is far from trustworthy, as demonstrated when that ancient scientist dropped the wood and lead balls from the tower of Pisa. As he held the balls over the edge of the tower, surely the much greater pull on the hand holding the lead ball should have convinced him that the experiment was unnecessary; that no two bodies would behave the same. Even today, watching a feather and a lead shot fall through a vacuum is fascinating, because it is still "unexpected" or counterintuitive.

Perhaps it is this same sense of the unexpected that has fascinated those of us who are working in this new area now called software science. The first experimental results were obtained nearly five years ago; since that time the methods have been refined and extended in many unanticipated directions, but in each case further investigation has increased rather than limited confidence in the results.

Credit for the intellectual encouragement essential to those of us who have pursued these investigations belongs to many perceptive individuals, the foremost of whom is Dr. Richard Hamming of Bell Laboratories and the Naval Postgraduate School. His quick understanding served as a most important catalyst.

Further encouragement, and financial support has come not only from the National Science Foundation under which the work was initiated, but also from the Research Laboratories of General Motors, and International Business Machines' Research Laboratory at San Jose. It is a pleasure to be able to acknowledge a debt to Drs. Donald Hart and George Dodd of GM, and to Drs. Leonard Liu, Frank King and Frank Palermo and their colleagues at IBM who made my sabbatical there so profitable.

The insights added by post-colloquia discussions have also been important to the development of the field, and while they are perhaps less tangible, they definitely deserve acknowledgment. This is particularly true in the case of Professors William Huggins and Gerard Meyers of Johns Hopkins, Dr. Gene Ritter of the Naval Ordinance Laboratory, Professor Larry Symes of the University of Regina, Professor Donald Knuth of Stanford, Professors Roger Roman and Rodney Oldhoeft of Arizona State, Professor Robert Rosin of Iowa State, Professor Marshall Yovits of Ohio State, and the Computer Science faculties and graduate students at the universities of Illinois, Indiana, Saskatchewan, California, and Toronto. In like manner, I am indebted to the faculty and students at Purdue, most especially Professors Sam Conte, Dave Workman, Victor Schneider and Paul Young, each of whom often contributed the essential question at its proper time.

Of course, their support of such research or suggestions for its improvement can not be inferred to cover any errors in the diverse material presented here.

The list of scientists participating through their signed works, adding both knowledge and stature to the field, and making this monograph possible, currently includes:

Rudolf Bayer	Jose Ingojo
Technical University—Munich	*Purdue University*
Robert Bohrer	Dale Kennedy
University of Illinois	*University of Nebraska*
Necdet Bulut	Gerald Kulm
Middle East University, Ankara	*Purdue University*
Atilla Elci	Daniel Ostapko
Middle East University, Ankara	*IBM—Poughkeepsie*
James Elshoff	Karl Ottenstein
General Motors	*Purdue University*
Yasuo Funami	J. E. Sullivan
Fuji Bank, Tokyo	*Mitre*
Ronald Gordon	Paul Zislis
Purdue University	*Bell Labs*
J. C. Harvill	Stuart Zweben
Southern Methodist University	*Ohio State University*

In addition to offering the proper place for acknowledgments, a preface traditionally requires a definition of the audience for whom a book is written. Since an author might otherwise write a book for himself, the tradition is a good one, but in this case somewhat difficult to fulfill. This is due in part to the extremely wide applicability of the results presented.

It now seems that anyone whose work concerns man as a symbol manipulator has sufficient material of interest available. Most of the concepts are not new in any absolute sense, but only newly quantified and it is quantification that enables man to find the relationships allowing him to transform an art or a craft into a science. Because symbol manipulation is a component of so many arts, the audience is difficult to define.

For the computer professional, whether a practicing programmer, project manager, or research professor, this monograph offers a rational approach to the solution of several important problems. These include the prediction of programming requirements for proposed projects, the prediction of initial error rates, the quantitative evaluation of programming languages, the effect of modularity, and a method for measuring the differences between programs written by experts and those written by novices.

Further applications of the basic material presented in part I beyond those discussed in part II may also be expected. For example, a simple mechanical method for detecting plagiarism in computer programs has been implemented and tested by Karl Ottenstein, building upon the work of Necdet Bulut. Paul Zislis used the concepts presented in part I of this monograph to mechanically partition previously written computer programs into individually meaningful parts. His primary objective was to provide a tool for use in the testing of large programs, but the technique also suggests an approach to the problem of decompilation or mechanical abstracting. (Citations to these works appear in the references.)

For the psychologist, the material in chapter 12 on modularity suggests a possible tie-in, and of course the material on the mental effort of programming may most properly belong to psychology. While the derivation in chapter 8 employs the Stroud Number from psychology, clearly its value could have been determined from the programming experiments themselves.

Kennedy and Bruning, in a most interesting experiment in child development psychology, have already found a use for the measure of level discussed in chapter 5, and apparently for the dual concepts of intelligence content and potential volume as well.

For the linguist, the results of chapter 13 should be quite useful. While the "Zipf-Mandelbrot Law" of word frequency distributions is not mentioned explicitly in that chapter, Stuart Zweben has shown that operator frequencies should, and do, follow a modified Zipf's Law, but that operand frequencies should not, and do not. This finding for computer program language is apparently in complete agreement with a similar finding of Miller, Newman and Friedman for the English language. The importance of chapter 13, however, does not lie in distribution laws, which may have more intellectual interest than practical value. Instead, it demonstrates that deeper relations do exist, and that these have a high potential utility.

For the expert in mathematical education, or perhaps even *the educational generalist,* the combination of chapter 13 with the material of part I should prove interesting. Gerald Kulm demonstrated that quantitative measures of level and content may be of value in assessing comprehensibility for text evaluation. As the reader may already suspect, such tests have not been applied to this monograph itself. In fact, the only place in which the results discussed in the monograph were applied to the writing of the monograph was in chapter 10, where mathematical simplification was accomplished by removing all instances of the impurity classes of chapter 7.

With respect to reference citations, an unconventional style was adopted: a proper bibliographic entry appears in the list of references for every case in which an author's name appears in the text, but explicit indexing or keying is omitted. Since it is intended that the monograph be essentially self-contained, this convention should benefit most readers.

As for claims of correctness, one can of course make none. Just as in all other fields of natural science, we must expect that future understanding will exceed that of the present. A theory, unlike a theorem, is subject to constant change as knowledge increases, but even to be called a theory, any hypothesis must pass many tests. Perhaps it is worth remembering that only when an hypothesis fails is humankind in a position to learn something new.

                                       M. H. HALSTEAD

West Lafayette, Indiana
August 3, 1976

Part I BASIC PROPERTIES
AND THEIR RELATIONS

Starting in 1972, several quantitative relationships have been reported that appear to have general applicability to the writing or implementation of computer programs, and to some extent to technical prose as well. The material on this newly recognized discipline has appeared in widely scattered technical reports, journal articles, conference proceedings, and doctoral theses under such diverse headings as "thermodynamics of algorithms," "algorithm dynamics," "software physics," and "software theory."

It is the purpose of Part I of this monograph to provide a systematic and unified treatment of that part of this theory which is presently known, or thought to be known. A complete list of references, both to that part of the general scientific literature cited, and to the works of the many individuals who have contributed to software science, appear at the conclusion, with only casual mention in the textual material itself.

LIST OF SYMBOLS

D	Difficulty $(1/L)$	$V*$	Potential volume
E	Effort	$V**$	Boundary volume
f	Frequency	β	Block size (Greek beta)
I	Intelligence content	η	Vocabulary size
k	Redundancy factor		(Greek eta)
L	Program level	η_1	Unique operator count
M	Number of modules	η_2	Unique operand count
N	Program length	$\eta*$	Potential vocabulary
N_1	Total operators	η_1*	Potential operator count
N_2	Total operands	η_2*	Potential operand count
T	Implementation	λ	Language level
	time		(Greek lambda)
V	Program volume	ν	Branch count (Greek nu)

FREQUENTLY USED EQUATIONS

$$\eta = \eta_1 + \eta_2$$

$$N = N_1 + N_2$$

$$\eta = k\eta'$$

$$\eta* = \eta_1* + \eta_2* = 2 + \eta_2*$$

$$\hat{N} = \eta_1 \log_2 \eta_1 + \eta_2 \log_2 \eta_2$$

$$V = N \log_2 \eta$$

$$V* = \eta* \log_2 \eta*$$

$$L = V*/V$$

$$\hat{L} = \frac{\eta_1*}{\eta_1} \frac{\eta_2}{N_2} = \frac{2}{\eta_1} \frac{\eta_2}{N_2}$$

$$I = \hat{L}V \simeq V*$$

$$\lambda = LV* = L^2V$$

$$E = V/L = V^2/V*$$

$$T = E/S$$

Chapter 1

Introduction

Software Science is a recently discovered field of the natural sciences that is presently still in the exploratory stage of development. It is concerned initially with algorithms and their implementation, either as computer programs, or as instruments of human communication. As an experimental science, it deals only with those properties of algorithms that can be measured, either directly or indirectly, statically or dynamically, and with the relationships among those properties that remain invariant under translation from one language to another.

The investigations that led to the discovery of this branch of physical science were motivated by the recognized need of Computer Science in general, and Software Engineering in particular, for a substantial foundation in theoretical and experimental science. To some extent this requirement may have been met, with the derivation and experimental validation of relationships that appear to govern the implementation of algorithms, with respect to their length, their level, their modularity, purity, volume, intelligence content, and the number of mental discriminations and time required to write them.

If one considers an algorithm to be a distillation of human thought, then it follows that governing relationships most easily observed in highly stylized computer language should apply in other media of expression as well. While this cannot yet be accepted with any confidence, preliminary work in electronic circuitry, in technical English prose, and in psychology indicates that this may be true. The potential application of software science to such diverse areas will be discussed in Part II, even though the subject matter in Part I will be developed solely with respect to computer programs. It should also be mentioned, because in the past computer programs have most often been studied from the point of view of mathematics, that the approach used relies upon the experimental validation of relationships rather than on the proof of theorems. Consequently, as in any branch of natural science, any theory developed or any laws discovered, may be relied upon only within the region in which they have been tested.

Software science does share one common boundary with Information Theory, but the two should not be confused. Instead, one may now

accept the arguments expressed by D. M. MacKay in 1950, to the effect
that Shannon's fundamental contributions should be called "Communi-
cation-Information Theory", and that we should still seek what MacKay
called "Scientific-Information Theory". A similar view was expressed
by the distinguished academician Liapunov in 1959, when, after noting
Shannon's work, he envisioned a "future" development of a "General
Metric Theory of Algorithms" in the following statement:

> Описанные работы представляют собой первые шаги в области
> математических задач кибернетики. Они обьединены некой общей
> направленностью замыслов, которую можно характеризовать
> как начало разработки общей метрической теории алгоритмов
> или теории алгоритмов с оценками. Однако построение такой
> теории является еще делом будущего.

THE IDEALIZED SOFTWARE CYCLE

In principle, an algorithm implemented in any given language, say
Fortran, can be subjected to four distinct processes without altering its
inherent quality. It can be compiled or subjected to the process of
translation from a higher level to a lower level language, such as assembly language or machine language. It can be optimized with respect
to any given machine language: It can be subjected to the inverse
compilation process: decompilation, that is, a translation from lower level
to higher level language. The implementation of an algorithm can, finally
be expanded, or changed to a canonical form by unwinding loops, replacing calls on procedures by the procedures themselves, and reversing
the process of optimization.

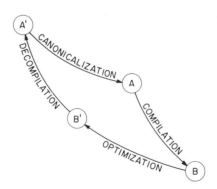

Figure 1.1   The Idealized Software Cycle

In principle these four processes could be combined in a cyclic operation as shown in figure 1.1. If no information were lost, then an implementation of an algorithm would return to a condition identical to the initial condition after being processed through the cycle any number of times. Since neither the optimization nor the inverse compilation process can be both rigorous and practical simultaneously, a loss of information is to be expected. Consequently, the cycle of figure 1.1 must be considered as idealized, in the same sense as, in thermodynamics, a frictionless (hence ideal) heat engine would follow the cycle of Carnot.

Any translation between language A and language B must consist of some combination of processes making up this idealized cycle.

COORDINATES

At this point, we note that figure 1.1 lacks an important attribute: no x-y coordinates are given. Measurable properties of expressions of algorithms must be found, so that the quantitative relationship between points A and B can be determined. Otherwise the very concept of a software cycle would be too abstract to serve any scientific purpose.

Clearly, such coordinates, or any other metrics for the study of implementations or expressions of algorithms in various languages should not be directly related to the execution of an algorithm, because only the machine language versions can be directly executed. Consequently, the basic metrics of any algorithm must be obtainable directly from a static expression of that algorithm in any language.

Given an implementation of the algorithm in any language, it is possible to identify all of the operands, defined as variables or constants, that the implementation employs. Similarly, it is also possible to identify all of the operators, defined as symbols or combinations of symbols that affect the value or ordering of an operand. From the identification of operators and operands, it is possible to define a number of countable, hence measurable, entities that must be present in any version of any algorithm. These properties are the basic metrics from which the relationships of software science have been obtained.

MEASURABLE PROPERTIES OF ALGORITHMS

Properties of any expression of any algorithm (or computer program), that are capable of being counted or measured, include the following:

η_1 = number of unique or distinct *operators* appearing in that implementation.

η_2 = number of unique or distinct *operands* appearing in that implementation.

N_1 = total usage of all of the *operators* appearing in that implementation.

N_2 = total usage of all of the *operands* appearing in that implementation.

$f_{1,j}$ = number of occurrences of the *j*th most frequently occurring operator, where $j = 1, 2, \ldots , \eta_1$.

$f_{2,j}$ = number of occurrences of the *j*th most frequently used operand, where $j = 1, 2, \ldots , \eta_2$.

From these basic metrics, it is convenient to define the *vocabulary* η as:

$$\eta = \eta_1 + \eta_2$$

and the implementation *length N* as:

$$N = N_1 + N_2$$

Further, from these definitions it is useful to note that the following three relationships must apply:

$$N_1 = \sum_{j=1}^{j=\eta_1} f_{1,j} \tag{1.1}$$

$$N_2 = \sum_{j=1}^{j=\eta_2} f_{2,j} \tag{1.2}$$

$$N = \sum_{i=1}^{i=2} \sum_{j=1}^{j=\eta_i} f_{i,j} \tag{1.3}$$

EXAMPLE: EUCLID'S ALGORITHM

To illustrate the metrics defined thus far and to provide a concrete example for material to be presented later, we will introduce here a sample program. The oldest known algorithm, that of Euclid for finding the greatest common divisor of two numbers, has, clearly, been expressed in most known languages, from the original Greek to the most recent computer languages. An implementation of the algorithm in an early form of Algol, as published by Clausen (in the Communications of the Association for Computing Machinery), has been copied directly as shown below.

```
        IF (A = 0)
LAST:   BEGIN GCD := B; RETURN END;
        IF (B = 0)
        BEGIN GCD := A; RETURN END;
HERE:   G := A/B; R:= A − B× G;
        IF (R=0) GO TO LAST;
        A := B; B := R; GO TO HERE
```

The software science parameters, obtained by classifying and counting, are given in Tables 1.1 and 1.2. With respect to the classification of operators, it is intuitively obvious that the replacement symbol $:=$, the equality sign $=$, subtraction $-$, division $/$, and multiplication $\times$ conform to the usual definition of operators. A bit of reflection should confirm that the classification of an opening and closing parenthesis pair is as a single grouping operator. Since the BEGIN...END pair performs an identical grouping function, it is also classified as the same operator. Since the labels HERE: and LAST: are neither variables nor constants, they are not operands. They must, therefore, be operators or parts of operators. The combination of the instruction GO TO HERE and the label

Table 1.1
Operator Parameters: Greatest Common Divisor Algorithm

Operator	j	$f_{1,j}$
;	1	9
:=	2	6
( ) or BEGIN...END	3	5
IF	4	3
=	5	3
/	6	1
−	7	1
×	8	1
GO TO HERE	9	1
GO TO LAST	10	1
	$\eta_1 = 10$	$N_1 = 31$

Table 1.2
Operand Parameters: Greatest Common Divisor Algorithm

Operand	j	$f_{2,j}$
B	1	6
A	2	5
O	3	3
R	4	3
G	5	2
GCD	6	2
	$\eta_2 = 6$	$N_2 = 21$

HERE: determines program flow by determining a program counter or text pointer; consequently, the combination is classified as one operator. An unused label, on the other hand, is treated as if it were only a comment, hence not essential to, or part of, the program. The delimiter, or semicolon, also determines program flow, merely by advancing it, hence the semicolon is also classified as an operator. For the same reason, all control structures, such as IF, IF...THEN....ELSE, or DO...WHILE are classified as operators. Note that the ability to define labeled points, like the ability to define new functions, removes any limitation on the growth of η_1 that might otherwise be imposed by the instruction set of a machine, or the design of a language.

The classification of operands, as illustrated in Table 1.2, is intuitively obvious, and requires no further explanation.

The concept that *an algorithm consists of operators and operands, and of nothing else* is most easily verified by considering simple digital computers whose instruction format consists of only two parts: an operation code and an operand address. Generalization to computer oriented languages is simply by induction, but the further generalization to verbs as operators and nouns as operands in natural language requires more caution, and additional insight from linguistics, as we shall find in Chapter 13.

In the chapters that follow we will explain and demonstrate the various ways in which the parameters thus far obtained have been used in the quantitative analysis of computer programs and other forms of expression.

Chapter 2

Program Length

The first equation found to hold among the software parameters defined in the previous chapter was a quantitative relationship that exists between length N and vocabulary η. Initially, it was not merely unexpected, but generally counter-intuitive. Understanding of this result has improved with time, however, so that now we can provide some explanation for its existence, in addition to conclusive experimental evidence that the relationship does in fact apply.

While the length relationship has been found to be of real value in solving more complex problems; these uses are discussed in later chapters. Similarly, its validity for noncomputer languages, such as technical English, will be treated separately in Chapter 13.

A string of length N made up of items from a vocabulary of η different items must obey a number of constraints. Trivially, the condition that each of the η items must appear at least once guarantees that:

$$\eta \leq N \qquad (2.1)$$

so that there is a lower limit on N in terms of η.

On the other hand, if one additional condition is met, then there will also be an upper limit. This limit may be found in the following way. Divide the string of length N into substrings of length η. Thus divided, a computer program would consist of N/η statements each of length η. Similarly, an English passage thus treated would consist of N/η sentences each of length η. Now, if the string is required to obey the single condition that it contain no two identical substrings of length η, then an upper limit will exist. The condition that there be no duplications of substrings of length η appears most reasonable for computer programs, in which economy of expression requires that a common subexpression be given a distinct name, so that it need be evaluated only once. Consequently, if a common subexpression of length η should be needed by the program more than once, assigning it to a unique operand would have the effect of increasing η by one.

The number of possible combinations of η things taken η at a time is well known, and can be shown inductively as follows:

9

$\eta = 1$ $\eta = 2$ $\eta = 3$

$\eta = 1$	$\eta = 2$	$\eta = 3$		
(1) *A*	(1) *AA*	(1) *AAA*	(10) *BAA*	(19) *CAA*
	(2) *AB*	(2) *AAB*	(11) *BAB*	(20) *CAB*
	(3) *BA*	(3) *AAC*	(12) *BAC*	(21) *CAC*
	(4) *BB*	(4) *ABA*	(13) *BBA*	(22) *CBA*
		(5) *ABB*	(14) *BBB*	(23) *CBB*
		(6) *ABC*	(15) *BBC*	(24) *CBC*
		(7) *ACA*	(16) *BCA*	(25) *CCA*
		(8) *ACB*	(17) *BCB*	(26) *CCB*
		(9) *ACC*	(18) *BCC*	(27) *CCC*

$1 = 1^1$ $4 = 2^2$ $27 = 3^3 = \eta^{\eta}$

Consequently, a program could consist of at most η^{η} substrings of length η, giving the upper limit:

$$N \leqslant \eta^{\eta+1} \tag{2.2}$$

Now the upper limit of equation (2.2) may be further refined by noting that the vocabulry η consists of both operators η_1 and operands η_2, and operands and operators tend to alternate. For an η of four, consisting of 2 operators and 2 operands, despite the fact that $4^4 = 256$, there would only be the following possible combinations:

(1) AaAa	(5) AaAb	(9) AbAa	(13) AbAb
(2) AaBa	(6) AaBb	(10) AbBa	(14) AbBb
(3) BaAa	(7) BaAb	(11) BbAa	(15) BbAb
(4) BaBa	(8) BaBb	(12) BbBa	(16) BbBb

Consequently, equation (2.2) may be replaced by:

$$N \leqslant \eta \times \eta_1^{\eta_1} \times \eta_2^{\eta_2} \tag{2.3}$$

Now the upper limit of equation (2.3) must include not only the single ordered set of N elements that is the program we seek, but it must also contain all possible subsets of that ordered set. Fortunately, the family of all possible subsets of a set of N elements is so well-known that it has a name, "The Power Set", and this family itself has 2^N elements. Consequently, we may equate the number of possible combinations of operators and operands with the number of elements in the power set, and solve for the length of an implementation of an algorithm in terms of its vocabulary. From

$$2^N = \eta_1{}^{\eta_1} \times \eta_2{}^{\eta_2} \tag{2.4}$$

we have

$$N = \log_2 (\eta_1{}^{\eta_1} \times \eta_2{}^{\eta_2}) \tag{2.5}$$

or

$$N = \log_2 \eta_1{}^{\eta_1} + \log_2 \eta_2{}^{\eta_2} \tag{2.6}$$

yielding the length equation

$$\hat{N} = \eta_1 \log_2 \eta_1 + \eta_2 \log_2 \eta_2 \tag{2.7}$$

where the "hat" has been placed on N to distinguish the quantity obtained, the calculated length, with this equation from the value of the length N obtained by direct observation.

Regardless of how reasonably or simply equation (2.7) was derived, the nature of experimental science requires that it be validated quantitatively before it can be accepted. Even then, of course, it must be recognized as only an approximation to reality, subject to refinement as knowledge increases.

Applying equation (2.7) to the GCD example of Chapter 1, for which $\eta_1 = 10$, $\eta_2 = 6$, and

$$N = N_1 + N_2 = 31 + 21 = 52$$

gives:

$$\hat{N} = 10 \log_2 10 + 6 \log_2 6 = 33 + 16 = 49$$

Clearly, the sample algorithm was written in such a way that $\hat{N}$ fell within 10% of N. But just as clearly, it could have been written in an infinite number of ways for which the relationship would not have been true. For example, in the last line, the value of B would have remained unchanged even if it had been alternately multiplied by R and divided by R a thousand times, thereby increasing N by 4000 without changing η. The interesting implications of this paradox will be investigated in a later chapter, after some additional properties have been studied. In the meantime, let us consider how equation (2.7) may be tested.

TESTING THE LENGTH EQUATION

A sample of programs to be tested should be chosen with as much objectivity as possible. This suggests selecting a group of previously

Table 2.1
Observed length N vs calculated length $\hat{N}$
From Equation (2.7) for Algorithms (1) through (14) of *CACM*

Algorithm number	N	$\hat{N}$	Algorithm Number	N	$\hat{N}$
(1)	104	104	(8)	131	117
(2)	82	77	(9)	314	288
(3)	453	300	(10)	46	52
(4)	132	139	(11)	53	52
(5)	123	123	(12)	59	62
(6)	98	101	(13)	59	57
(7)	59	62	(14)	186	163

published algorithms, and after selecting the group, omitting none of them. Further, the relationship should be validated first for small programs, lest unknown effects of modularity mask the basic relationship. Also, since the relationship is expected to apply to well-organized, non-redundant algorithms, the first sample should consist of programs written by experts, who might be expected to reduce their programs to polished form before publication. A sample set meeting these criteria can be obtained by selecting the first dozen algorithms published in the Algorithm section of the *Communications of the Association for Computing Machinery*, when that section was initiated in 1961. The results of analyzing this sample are shown in Table 2.1.

The data of Table 2.1 have been plotted in figure 2.1, where it is apparent that, with the exception of algorithm (3) (this exception will be understood later), $\hat{N}$ yields a rather close estimate of algorithm length from a simple function of the vocabulary used in it. Further, the agreement for these programs could not be improved materially by inserting arbitrary constants to change either the slope or the intercept.

It has long been realized in any natural science, however, that any important relationship observed experimentally in one laboratory must be shown to be independently reproducible in another laboratory before it can be accepted. Robert Bohrer of the University of Illinois was the first investigator to obtain an independent confirmation of the length equation. In February 1975, in the Eighth Annual Computer Science–Statistics Interface Proceedings, Bohrer published the results of his analysis of the first 13 algorithms in *Applied Statistics*. The statistics that Bohrer re-

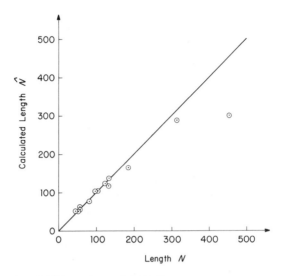

Figure 2.1   CACM Algorithms (1)–(14) [N vs $\eta_1 \log_2 \eta_1 + \eta_2 \log_2 \eta_2$]

ported for these 13 algorithms and for the 14 algorithms already discussed are reproduced in Table 2.2.

Bohrer's analysis demonstrated the reproducibility of the experimental validation of the length equation for a comparable set of algorithms. Like the ACM set, Bohrer selected the first 13 algorithms published in a given journal, and measured all of them. They were of roughly the same length, ($N = 205$ against $N = 136$), and the algorithms were published in Fortran rather than Algol.

As Table 2.2 shows, the length equation agreed within 1% for Bohrer's sample, although the mean squared error (MSE) was larger than for the

Table 2.2
Bohrer's Independent Verification of the Length Equation

	ACM (14 *Algorithms*)			AS (13 *Algorithms*)		
	Mean	(MSE)	(RMSE)	Mean	(MSE)	(RMSE)
N	135.6	12360.	111.	205.1	6952	83.
$N - \hat{N}$	14.3	1568.	39.6	5.0	1089	33.0
$(N - \hat{N})/N$	0.030	0.012	0.109	0.010	0.028	0.168

Note. MSE is mean squared error; RMSE is square root of mean squared error.

ACM sample. If one ascribes the usual meaning to the square root of the mean squared error (RMSE), then it would appear that 83% to 89% of the variation in algorithm length is coupled with variations in η_1 and η_2.

VALIDATION OF THE LENGTH RELATION
WITH LARGER SAMPLES

The Computing Center of Purdue University had in 1974 a library of programs, 429 of which were written completely in Fortran. A program, which was in many respects like a compiler, was written to process these 429 source programs, in order to obtain individual measurements of η_1, η_2, N_1, and N_2 from them. The total sample had a combined count of operator and operand usages of 242,990, with individual lengths varying over a range from 7 to 10,661. Table 2.3 summarizes the results, where each pair of values is the mean of 20 programs, except the last, which is the mean of the nine largest programs.

The coefficient of correlation between each of the 429 observed lengths and the lengths calculated with equation (2.7) is 0.95. Using the 20 program means of the first 400 programs (ignoring the 29 largest) increases the correlation coefficient to 0.993.

INDEPENDENT VALIDATION
FOR LONGER PROGRAMS

Just as Robert Bohrer of the University of Illinois was able to reproduce the results of the length equation experiment for a sample of

Table 2.3
Observed vs Estimated Lengths of 429 Fortran Programs
in Purdue University's Library

N	$\hat{N}$	N	$\hat{N}$	N	$\hat{N}$	N	$\hat{N}$
29	45	170	168	372	322	774	596
58	74	198	210	437	358	976	618
78	96	227	230	484	385	1287	878
97	115	264	240	549	389	2202	1553
121	125	301	264	612	435	5534	5417
146	146	331	274				

Table 2.4
Elshoff's Independent Validation of the Length
Equation for Commercial PL/I Programs

Class $2^i < N < 2^{i+1}$ i	Number of Programs in Class	Mean Values N	$\hat{N}$
14	3	18,592	19,091
13	17	10,685	11,049
12	23	5,751	6,005
11	39	3,165	3,318
10	17	1,590	1,663
9	11	831	911
8	4	369	522
7	5	198	195
6	1	122	129
Totals	120	41,303	42,883

small published programs, James Elshoff of General Motors Research Laboratories confirmed the validity of equation (2.7) for a large group of commercial programs. Elshoff's data consisted of 120 PL/I programs with a combined total of more than 100,000 PL/I statements. He then implemented a computer program, with which he automatically obtained values of η_1, η_2, N_1, and N_2. Elshoff then measured N and calculated $\hat{N}$ from equation (2.7). He reported a correlation between N and $\hat{N}$ of 0.98. His data are summarized by class intervals in Table 2.4.

The data from Tables 2.1 through 2.4 have been combined in figure 2.2, where it is clear that equation (2.7) gives a rather close agreement to program length over many orders of magnitude. Further, this agreement cannot be materially improved by inserting even arbitrary constants or coefficients into equation (2.7).

This finding gains significance when it is remembered that, for every way in which an algorithm can be implemented in agreement with equation (2.7), there are an infinite number of ways in which an equivalent version could be written. This suggests that the human brain obeys a more rigid set of rules than it has been aware of, and that the parameters η_1, η_2, N_1, and N_2 may serve as useful elements in eliciting further relationships.

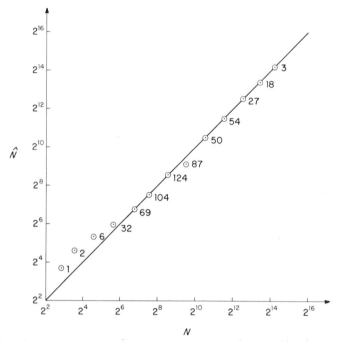

Figure 2.2 Data from 577 Programs [N vs $\eta_1 \log_2 \eta_1 + \eta_2 \log_2 \eta_2$]

Before accepting the length-vocabulary relationship, as it is approximated by the length equation, however, there is an even more general test that can be applied.

VALIDATION BY PARTS

Equation (2.7), which will be referred to henceforth simply as the length equation, is definitely nonlinear. Because of its nonlinearity, the fact that it appears to hold for complete programs in no way guarantees that it will also hold for parts of programs.

For example, consider a program of length $N = 48$, with vocabulary of $\eta = 16$ where $\eta_1 = \eta_2 = 8$, such that $\hat{N} = 48 = N$. Now assume that this program is divided into two parts, A and B, of equal lengths, so that $N_A = 24$ and $N_B = 24$.

Now, if both parts each employed all of the operators and operands of the original or complete program, then the length equation would yield

$$\hat{N}_A = \hat{N}_B = 8 \log_2 8 + 8 \log_2 8 = 48$$

giving

$$\hat{N}_A + \hat{N}_B = 96$$

instead of

$$N = 48$$

On the other hand, if neither of the two parts contained any of the same operators or operands used in the other part, then

$$\eta_{1_A} = \eta_{1_B} = 4$$
$$\eta_{2_A} = \eta_{2_B} = 4$$

and

$$\hat{N}_A = \hat{N}_B = 4 \log_2 4 + 4 \log_2 4 = 16$$

giving

$$\hat{N}_A + \hat{N}_B = 32$$

instead of

$$N = 48$$

Consequently, with the condition that $\eta_{1_A} = \eta_{1_B} = \eta_{2_A} = \eta_{2_B}$, the only value for which the length calculated by parts would equal the proper value would require $\eta_A = 10.21$, or 64% of η.

There does not appear to be any *a priori* reason to expect that a logical modularization of a program into parts should conform to this relationship, nor is the length equation invalidated for complete programs if it does not conform. Nonetheless, if the phenomena were observed in modular programs, such that $N = \hat{N}$ for the parts as well as for the whole, then an even more basic property of the length relationship would be exposed.

This hypothesis has been tested by Jose Ingojo, who selected a small compiler as published in a computer textbook, in which each of its 14 modules was presented separately. He found that when the compiler was treated as a whole, the software values were

$$\eta_1 = 83$$
$$\eta_2 = 96$$
$$\hat{N} = 1161$$
$$N = 1334$$
$$\frac{N - \hat{N}}{N} = 0.13$$

The same compiler evaluated as 14 separate modules yielded the following data

$$\bar{\eta}_1 = \frac{1}{14} \sum_{i=1}^{i=14} {}_{1,i} = \frac{176}{14} = 12.6$$

$$\bar{\eta}_2 = \frac{1}{14} \sum_{i=1}^{i=14} \eta_{2,i} = \frac{193}{14} = 13.8$$

$$\hat{N} = 14(\bar{\eta}_1 \log_2 \bar{\eta}_1 + \bar{\eta}_2 \log_2 \bar{\eta}_2) = 14 \times 98.3 = 1376$$

$$N = 1334$$

$$\frac{N - \hat{N}}{N} = 0.031$$

Additionally, the correlation coefficient between the 14 pairs of N, $\hat{N}$ values is 0.988.

Consequently, it appears reasonable to assume that the vocabulary–length relationship governs the individual parts of a logically partitioned program as well as it does the program as a whole. This finding, in turn, lends even greater weight to the previously mentioned observation that the human brain must follow, or be governed by, an interesting set of rules of which it has (or we have) heretofore been unaware.

Looking again at the length equation, it appears that it may be interpreted in at least two ways. In the intuitively obvious interpretation, it does indeed represent the length of an expression of any algorithm. On the other hand, the sum of two logarithmic terms must also represent the product of multiplying those terms. Since the first term depends on operators, while the second depends on operands, the length may also be interpreted as two-dimensional, rather than scalar. Consequently, although N will continue to be referred to as a length, N may also be expected to behave like an area measure as well.

ꓳTENTIAL VOLUME V^*

The most succinct form in which an algorithm could ever be expressed ꓳuld require the prior existence of a language in which the required ꞏeration was already defined or implemented, perhaps as a subroutine procedure. In such a language, the implementation of that algorithm ꓳuld require nothing more than the naming of operands for its argu-ents and its resultants.

Denoting the corresponding parameters in an algorithm's shortest pos-ꞏle or most succinct form by starring them, it follows from equation .1) that the minimal, or *potential volume* V^* is

$$V^* = (N_1^* + N_2^*) \log_2(\eta_1^* + \eta_2^*) \tag{3.2}$$

Now in its minimal form, neither operators nor operands could require petition, thus

$$N_1^* = \eta_1^*$$

ꓐd

$$N_2^* = \eta_2^*$$

ꞏving

$$V^* = (\eta_1^* + \eta_2^*) \log_2(\eta_1^* + \eta_2^*) \tag{3.3}$$

ꞏurthermore, the minimum possible number of operators η_1^* for any ꞏgorithm is known. It must consist of one distinct operator for the name ꞏ the function or procedure and another to serve as an assignment or ꞏouping symbol. Therefore,

$$\eta_1^* = 2$$

ꞏquation (3.3) then becomes

$$V^* = (2 + \eta_2^*) \log_2(2 + \eta_2^*) \tag{3.4}$$

ꞏhere η_2^*, for small algorithms at least, should represent the number of ꞏifferent input/output parameters.

A significant consequence of equation (3.4) lies in the fact that the ꞏotential volume V^* of any algorithm should be independent of any ꞏanguage in which it might be expressed. Provided that η_2^* is evaluated ꞏs the number of conceptually unique operands involved, V^* appears to ꞏe a most useful measure of an algorithm's content.

Chapter 3

Program Volume

An important characteristic of an algorithm is its size. Whene
algorithm is translated from one language to another, its si
Similarly, in any one language some algorithms are smaller 1
To study such changes in a quantitative way requires tha
measurable quantity.

Furthermore, the size metric must be capable of application
variety of possible languages without losing either generalit
tivity. Consequently, it should be independent of the characte1
express an algorithm. Therefore the size metric should not
number of characters actually used to represent operand name
tors.

This problem can be solved by noting that for any particula1
is an absolute minimum length for the representation of 1
operator or operand name, if it is expressed in binary digits o
length depends only on the number of elements in the voc;
η. For example, a vocabulary of eight different elements rec
different designators, or the number of possible combinations
number having three digits. More generally, $\log_2 \eta$ is the
length in bits of all of the individual elements in a program.

A suitable metric for the size of any implementation of any
called the *volume V* can be defined as

$$V = N \log_2 \eta$$

where N is its length (or $N_1 + N_2$), and η is its vocabulary (or
This interpretation gives program volume the dimension of b

Clearly, if a given algorithm is translated from one language
its volume will be changed. For example, if an algorithm is
from Fortran to the machine code of some particular compute
volume will increase. On the other hand, an algorithm m
pressable in a more powerful language than the one it is 1
in which case the volume would be reduced. This latter possi1
considerable importance, and is treated separately here.

19

Chapter 3

Program Volume

An important characteristic of an algorithm is its size. Whenever a given algorithm is translated from one language to another, its size changes. Similarly, in any one language some algorithms are smaller than others. To study such changes in a quantitative way requires that *size* be a measurable quantity.

Furthermore, the size metric must be capable of application to the wide variety of possible languages without losing either generality or objectivity. Consequently, it should be independent of the character set used to express an algorithm. Therefore the size metric should not reflect the number of characters actually used to represent operand names or operators.

This problem can be solved by noting that for any particular case there is an absolute minimum length for the representation of the longest operator or operand name, if it is expressed in binary digits or bits. This length depends only on the number of elements in the vocabulary, or η. For example, a vocabulary of eight different elements requires eight different designators, or the number of possible combinations of a binary number having three digits. More generally, $\log_2 \eta$ is the minimum length in bits of all of the individual elements in a program.

A suitable metric for the size of any implementation of any algorithm, called the *volume V* can be defined as

$$V = N \log_2 \eta \qquad (3.1)$$

where N is its length (or $N_1 + N_2$), and η is its vocabulary (or $\eta_1 + \eta_2$). This interpretation gives program volume the dimension of bits.

Clearly, if a given algorithm is translated from one language to another, its volume will be changed. For example, if an algorithm is translated from Fortran to the machine code of some particular computer, then its volume will increase. On the other hand, an algorithm may be expressable in a more powerful language than the one it is written in, in which case the volume would be reduced. This latter possibility is of considerable importance, and is treated separately here.

POTENTIAL VOLUME V^*

The most succinct form in which an algorithm could ever be expressed would require the prior existence of a language in which the required operation was already defined or implemented, perhaps as a subroutine or procedure. In such a language, the implementation of that algorithm would require nothing more than the naming of operands for its arguments and its resultants.

Denoting the corresponding parameters in an algorithm's shortest possible or most succinct form by starring them, it follows from equation (3.1) that the minimal, or *potential volume V^** is

$$V^* = (N_1^* + N_2^*) \log_2 (\eta_1^* + \eta_2^*) \tag{3.2}$$

Now in its minimal form, neither operators nor operands could require repetition, thus

$$N_1^* = \eta_1^*$$

and

$$N_2^* = \eta_2^*$$

giving

$$V^* = (\eta_1^* + \eta_2^*) \log_2 (\eta_1^* + \eta_2^*) \tag{3.3}$$

Furthermore, the minimum possible number of operators η_1^* for any algorithm is known. It must consist of one distinct operator for the name of the function or procedure and another to serve as an assignment or grouping symbol. Therefore,

$$\eta_1^* = 2$$

Equation (3.3) then becomes

$$V^* = (2 + \eta_2^*) \log_2 (2 + \eta_2^*) \tag{3.4}$$

where η_2^*, for small algorithms at least, should represent the number of different input/output parameters.

A significant consequence of equation (3.4) lies in the fact that the potential volume V^* of any algorithm should be independent of any language in which it might be expressed. Provided that η_2^* is evaluated as the number of conceptually unique operands involved, V^* appears to be a most useful measure of an algorithm's content.

Returning to the sample program of Euclid's Algorithm (Chapter 1), we have, for its volume:

$$V = (N_1 + N_2) \log_2 (\eta_1 + \eta_2)$$
$$= (31 + 21) \log_2 (10 + 6)$$
$$= 208 \text{ bits}$$

To find its potential volume, we only need a count of the input and output parameters which are required. In this case, these are A, B, and R, so that $\eta_2^* = 3$. The potential volume is then

$$V^* = (\eta_1^* + \eta_2^*) \log_2 (\eta_1^* + \eta_2^*)$$
$$= (2 + \eta_2^*) \log_2 (2 + \eta_2^*)$$
$$= (2 + 3) \log_2 (2 + 3)$$
$$= 11.6 \text{ bits}$$

As mentioned earlier, if an algorithm is translated from one language to another the potential volume V^* will not change, but the actual volume V will increase or decrease depending upon the relative powers of the languages involved. It is easy to observe, however, that there cannot be a smooth transition from an expression in potential language, for which $V = V^*$, to any less powerful language, for which $V > V^*$. This abrupt transition at the boundary results from the condition that for a potential language, $N^* = \eta^*$, while for all other languages, the length equation applies, and $N > \eta$. Consequently, it is convenient to define a third volume, called the *boundary volume* V^{**}

$$V^{**} = (\eta_1^* \log_2 \eta_1^* + \eta_2^* \log_2 \eta_2^*) \log_2 (\eta_1^* + \eta_2^*) \quad (3.5)$$

or, since

$$\eta_1^* = 2 = \eta_1^* \log_2 \eta_1^*$$
$$V^{**} = (2 + \eta_2^* \log_2 \eta_2^*) \log_2 (2 + \eta_2^*) \quad (3.6)$$

Later in Chapter 8, Programming Effort, we will find that a deeper and more significant interpretation of program volume is also possible; but until then we only need to consider volume as a measure having the dimensions of binary digits or bits.

Chapter 4

Relations between Operators and Operands

The question of how the number of unique operators η_1 will vary with the number of unique operands η_2 as a given algorithm is expressed in languages of decreasing power is of considerable interest in its own right. This concept is of even more importance, however, when used in predicting other properties.

If we consider a wide range of different algorithms, all expressed in potential form, then it may be observed that although η_1^* remains constant and equal to two for each, η_2^* will vary over a wide range. Consequently, the value of η_2^* for a given algorithm determines the initial ratio of operands to operators. But as the total vocabulary η increases, the effect on η_1 must be greater than on η_2 if η_2^* is large.

The quantitative relationship that exists can be derived as follows. Starting from the vocabulary definition

$$\eta = \eta_1 + \eta_2 \tag{4.1}$$

and assuming that η_2 is a function of η_1 and η^*, where η_1 and η^* are independent, differentiating yields

$$\frac{d\eta}{d\eta_1} = 1 + \frac{d\eta_2}{d\eta_1} \tag{4.2}$$

Now if we set

$$\frac{d\eta}{d\eta_1} = \frac{V^{**}}{V^*} \tag{4.3}$$

where V^* is the potential volume and V^{**} is the boundary volume as defined by equation (3.6), equation (4.2) becomes

$$\frac{V^{**}}{V^*} - 1 = \frac{d\eta_2}{d\eta_1} \tag{4.4}$$

Integrating between limits

$$\int_{\eta_2^*}^{\eta_2} d\eta_2 = \frac{V^{**} - V^*}{V^*} \int_{\eta_1^*}^{\eta_1} d\eta_1 \tag{4.5}$$

yields

$$\eta_2 - \eta_2^* = \frac{V^{**} - V^*}{V^*} \, (\eta_1 - \eta_1^*) \tag{4.6}$$

Noting that $\eta_1^* = 2$, and solving for η_2

$$\eta_2 = \frac{V^{**} - V^*}{V^*} \, (\eta_1 - 2) + \eta_2^* \tag{4.7}$$

Setting

$$A = \frac{V^{**} - V^*}{V^*} \tag{4.8}$$

and

$$B = \eta_2^* - 2\frac{V^{**} - V^*}{V^*} \tag{4.9}$$

allows equation (4.7) to be written as

$$\eta_2 = A\eta_1 + B \tag{4.10}$$

where both A and B are single valued functions of η_2^*. This becomes more readily apparent when the definitions of V^* and V^{**} are substituted in equation (4.8). After algebraic simplification, equations (4.8) and (4.9) become

$$A = \frac{\eta_2^*}{\eta_2^* + 2} \log_2 \frac{\eta_2^*}{2} \tag{4.11}$$

and

$$B = \eta_2^* - 2A \tag{4.12}$$

Equation (4.6), or its equivalent equation (4.10), and through them, the assumption of equation (4.3), may be tested in the following way. Observations of the parameters η_2^*, η_1, and η_2 are available for fourteen Algol 58 algorithms and six PL/I algorithms. The published values are reproduced in Table 4.1. The values of η_2^* and η_1 may then be used to calculate an estimated value of η_2, called $\hat{\eta}_2$ from equation (4.10). A comparison of η_2 as observed for each of the 20 programs with $\hat{\eta}_2$ then provides an experimental test of the relationship.

The mean values of the observed and calculated operand counts agree, and their coefficient of correlation r is 0.994. As further evidence that equation (4.10) is an adequate representation of the observations, it is

Table 4.1
Experimental Verification of the Relation between
Input/Output Parameters η_2^*, and Unique Operators
η_1 and Operands η_2

	Observations			Calculated
Program number	η_2^*	η_1	η_2	$\hat{\eta}_2$
GM 36	68	47	329	290
GM 40	58	82	433	434
GM 28	43	49	214	242
GM 15	32	27	100	126
GM 50	32	35	168	156
ACM 3	12	18	41	47
ACM 9	10	19	41	43
ACM 1	8	10	18	21
ACM 14	7	15	25	25
GM 118	6	13	24	19
ACM 4	5	16	21	18
ACM 8	5	15	16	17
ACM 5	4	15	16	13
ACM 6	4	15	13	13
ACM 2	3	14	8	7
ACM 7	3	10	9	6
ACM 10	3	9	9	5
ACM 11	3	9	9	5
ACM 12	3	11	9	6
ACM 13	3	11	8	6
Means	22	76		75

interesting to note that while the correlation between η_1 and η_2 is also high, 0.975, the "unexplained variance" $1 - r^2$ is four times greater than that between η_2 and $\hat{\eta}_2$.

In several respects, this relationship between η and η^* is of even deeper significance than the relationship found earlier between η and N. This is because η^*, unlike η and N, depends only upon an inherent property of an algorithm, and not upon its implementation in any particular language.

Chapter 5

Program Level

Intuitively, the concept of the level at which a program might be written has been with us since the first "Higher-Level Languages" were referred to as such. Before a concept of this type can have much scientific utility, however, it must be reduced to quantitative or measurable terms. Until this has been done, it is not possible to measure the difference of this property between different expressions of an algorithm.

For example, once a given algorithm and a given language are decided on, alternative implementations may be comparatively ranked only on the basis of expert opinion, or perhaps by opinionated experts. Yet it is quite true that the level of implementation is vitally important in programming, because it contributes to the effort of writing, propensity for error, and ease of understanding.

In order to obtain suitable metrics for this property, it is necessary to note that the level of a language and the level of a program are distinctly different properties, even though they are closely related. This functional relationship, and the measurement of language level itself will be discussed later in Chapter 9. Here, we restrict the discussion to the measurement of the level of individual programs.

Now the definitions of program volume V and of potential volume V^* in Chapter 3 suggest a simple method of reducing this concept to quantitative form. By defining the *program level L* of the implementation of an algorithm as

$$L = \frac{V^*}{V} \tag{5.1}$$

it follows that only the most succinct expression possible for an algorithm can have a level of unity. More voluminous implementations must have lower values of level, so that $L \leq 1$.

Rearranging equation (5.1) to separate the implementation independent term

$$V^* = L \times V \tag{5.2}$$

emphasizes the fact that when the volume goes up, the level goes down, and conversely. This, in turn, suggests the possibility of exploring further implications of program level.

Clearly, it is usually easier to write a call on a procedure than it is to write the procedure itself. From that point of view, a potential language ($L = 1$) would be the easiest to use. But the concept of a general purpose potential language implies that any procedure that might ever be needed would already be available. Since the number of such procedures is infinite, the task of becoming familiar with a mere list of them is also infinite.

Consequently, the implementation and use of potential, or level one, languages is not feasible for general purpose work. On the other hand, a special purpose potential language, such as Sabre for airline reservations or the Job Control Language (JCL) for an operating system, becomes quite feasible. The over-all problem here, then, is one of balancing language implementation and user learning effort against the user savings. The latter depends on the amount of work done in the particular area, as well as the reduction in volume. Relationships for the user effort involved will be derived in Chapter 8.

First, however, it should be noted that program level serves a dual role when applied to ease or difficulty of understanding. For a person who understands all of the terms employed, a concept may be grasped more quickly or easily the higher the level at which it is presented. On the other hand, in order to convey a given concept to a person less familiar with, or less fluent in, a specific area requires a greater volume, and a lower level. As the saying goes, A Word to the Wise is Sufficient, and for a person fluent in a language, the difficulty of comprehension varies inversely with the level.

It is this basic relationship that underlies the propensity of special interest groups to develop their own jargons, or special purpose subsets of their own native tongues. For example, consider a hypothetical case in which a number of surgeons are conferring on a medical matter in the presence of a professor of English. While ten minutes might suffice for the information interchange amongst the medical men, the professor, more fluent in English than any of the others, might yet require an hour's explanation of what had been said. Substituting a group of truck-drivers, or even sports fans, for the surgeons would scarcely alter the ratio.

DERIVATION OF THE PROGRAM LEVEL RELATION

In the absence of a known value of potential volume V^*, it is often desirable to be able to obtain a measure of program level from an implementation directly, without reference to any possible procedure call

upon it. This may be accomplished by considering the separate effects of
operators and operands on the program level. With respect to operators,
it seems reasonable to assume that the greater the number of unique
operators employed in a given implementation, the lower the level of that
implementation.

Now the least possible number of unique operators that could ever be
employed is two, where the pair would consist of a function designator
and an assignment or grouping operator. This can be expressed as $\eta_1^* =
2$. On the other hand, there appears to be no limit to the number of
unique operators that might actually be employed, because they are not
limited by any language which permits the definition of new subpro-
cedures, subroutines, or transfers to labeled points.

From this, we have the proportionality

$$L \sim \frac{\eta_1^*}{\eta_1} \tag{5.3}$$

with respect to operators.

Operands, on the other hand, exhibit no unique minimum over all possible algorithms, so they must be treated differently. In their case, it
may suffice to note that whenever the name of an operand is repeated,
the repetition is an indication that the implementation is at a lower level.
This effect can be measured by taking the ratio of unique to total usage
of operands, giving the second proportionality

$$L \sim \frac{\eta_2}{N_2} \tag{5.4}$$

Combining equations (5.3) and (5.4), and noting that the constant of
proportionality must be unity, gives the program level equation

$$\hat{L} = \frac{\eta_1^*}{\eta_1} \frac{\eta_2}{N_2} \tag{5.5}$$

where the hat has been placed over the L to indicate that level measured
by equation (5.5) is an approximation to equation (5.1). Actually, of
course, it could be taken as an alternate definition of program level.
Experimental evidence suggests that either interpretation may be ac-
ceptable, as will be shown by the following analysis.

VALIDATION OF THE PROGRAM LEVEL EQUATION

Comparison of L with $\hat{L}$ requires a sample of implementations of
algorithms for which values of η_2^*, η_1, η_2, N_2, and N are available. As

noted in earlier chapters, all of these parameters except η_2^* may be obtained by direct count from a listing of any implementation. Obtaining values of η_2^*, however, will be slightly different. First, we note that η_2^* is defined as the number of *conceptually unique* arguments and results (or input and output parameters) required by a given algorithm. Consequently, for those cases in which an algorithm is implemented as a simple procedure, or as a subroutine, and for which a call on that procedure has also been written, the process is simple. In such a case, it is only necessary to count the parameters listed in the call, provided that result operand names are listed explicitly. For those cases in which a result operand is implied, rather than listed, it must still be counted. For example, the call

$$\sin (\Theta)$$

has an $\eta_2^* = 2$, just as it has if written as

$$\sin (\Theta S)$$

At this point it should be noted that the conceptually unique property of elements of η_2^* may be important. For example, the value of η_2^* would not be reduced by combining a number of input arguments into a single Goedel Number. Similarly, an input array should contain multiple values of a single operand, but in some cases it may not.

For those cases in which an algorithm is implemented as a straight routine to be executed directly, η_2^* must be determined in a different way. The method in this case consists of examining the implementation itself and counting all of the operands that are "busy-on-entry" or "busy-on-exit" from the implementation. There is some evidence to suggest that constants having a high information content, such as π, e, or Hastings coefficients may also contribute to η_2^* when they are internal to an implementation, as well as when they are introduced as input parameters. To simplify the procedure, however, the possible existence of internal contributors to η_2^* are ignored in the present analysis.

Algorithms (1) through (14) from the Communications of the Association for Computing Machinery (see Chapter 2) were published as procedures in Algol 58, and were accompanied by procedure calls. The observed software parameters, including η_2^* obtained from the calls, are taken from prior publications and are reproduced in Table 5.1. Six additional programs, for which values of η_2^* were obtained by "busy-on-entry" and "busy-on-exit" analysis have been published. These are also included in Table 5.1, greatly extending the range of program sizes.

Table 5.1
The Program Level Relationship

Algorithm Number		η_2^*	η_1	η_2	N_2	N	L	$\hat{L}$
			Observed Parameters				Level	
CACM	1	8	10	18	56	104	0.066	0.064
CACM	2	3	14	8	37	84	0.031	0.031
CACM	3	12	18	41	220	454	0.020	0.021
CACM	4	5	16	21	61	137	0.028	0.043
CACM	5	4	15	16	60	124	0.025	0.036
CACM	6	4	15	13	42	99	0.033	0.041
CACM	7	3	10	9	29	59	0.046	0.062
CACM	8	5	15	16	60	133	0.030	0.036
CACM	9	10	19	41	162	312	0.023	0.027
CACM	10	3	9	9	25	48	0.058	0.080
CACM	11	3	9	9	29	55	0.051	0.069
CACM	12	3	11	9	31	62	0.043	0.053
CACM	13	3	11	8	30	61	0.045	0.048
CACM	14	7	15	25	91	187	0.029	0.037
GM	15	32	27	100	301	686	0.036	0.025
GM	28	43	49	214	944	1919	0.016	0.009
GM	36	68	47	329	1318	2642	0.019	0.011
GM	40	58	82	433	1944	3985	0.010	0.005
GM	50	32	35	168	584	1248	0.018	0.016
GM	118	6	13	24	57	122	0.038	0.065
Mean							0.033	0.039
Coefficient of correlation								0.90

The penultimate column of Table 5.1 presents the calculation of program level according to the definition of equation (5.1), where V^* is obtained from η^* with equation (3.4), and V is obtained from N and $\eta = \eta_1 + \eta_2$ with equation (3.1). The last column of Table 5.1 gives the program level as calculated from η_1, η_2, N and $\eta_1^* = 2$ with equation (5.5).

Comparing the last two columns of Table 5.1 indicates that equations (5.1) and (5.5) do not yield identical results, which establishes that we are not dealing with a circular definition. On the other hand, the fact that the relationship derived with quite simple assumptions, equation

(5.5), agrees in general with the defining equation suggests that for many purposes L and $\hat{L}$ may be used interchangeably to specify the level at which a program has been implemented, at least for smaller programs.

Prediction of the level at which an algorithm could be implemented in a specified language, rather than how it has been implemented, however, depends not only on L, but also *language level* λ as will be shown in Chapter 9.

Chapter 6

Quantification of Intelligence Content

The relations for program volume and program level discussed in Chapters 4 and 5 suggest a rather fascinating possibility. If it is in fact true that the product of volume times level for any particular algorithm does not change as that algorithm is expressed in different languages, then it must represent a rather fundamental property of that algorithm. While it is intuitively clear that in machine language it requires a greater amount of detail to "say the same thing" than it does in PL/I, in the past we have had no way to measure "how much" has been said in either case. But now, if we merely postulate that any two equivalent programs do indeed "say the same thing", the question of "how much" may be answered.

It would seem that this fundamental measure of how much is said in a program should properly be called its *information content,* but the meaning of that term has been preempted by Shannon's Information Theory to refer only to the volume of a message, ignoring its level.

Solely to avoid confusing the literature with a second meaning for a useful term, we will substitute the rather presumptuous word "intelligence". The *intelligence content I* is then defined as

$$I = \hat{L} \times V \qquad (6.1)$$

This may be expanded, via equations (3.1) and (5.5), to become

$$I = \frac{2}{\eta_1} \frac{\eta_2}{N_2} \times (N_1 + N_2) \log_2 (\eta_1 + \eta_2) \qquad (6.2)$$

where all terms on the right-hand side are directly measurable from any expression of an algorithm. As reference to the previous chapter indicates, the intelligence content as calculated with equation (6.2) is approximately equal to, and highly correlated with, the potential volume V^* as given by equation (3.4). Consequently, since V^* is independent of the language in which an algorithm is expressed, the intelligence content I should also be independent.

This property of invariance under translation may be demonstrated by expressing Euclid's algorithm, the GCD of figure 1.2, in a range of different languages. Translations into PL/I, Fortran, and Compass (the assembly language of the CDC 6500) and corresponding frequency tables (Tables 6.1 through 6.3) have been published previously (by Zweben) and are reproduced below.

EUCLID'S ALGORITHM IN PL/I (*after Zweben*)

```
IF    A = 0    THEN
      LAST:   DO ;
              GCD = B ; RETURN ; END ;
IF    B = 0    THEN DO ;
              GCD = A ; RETURN ; END ;
      HERE:    G = A/B ;
/*    Assuming G to be integer variable */
      R = A − B * G ;
IF    R = 0 THEN GO TO   LAST ;
      A = B ; B = R ; GO TO HERE ;
```

Table 6.1
Frequency Counts of Euclid's Algorithm in PL/I (*after Zweben*)

j	Operator	$f_{1,j}$	j	Operand	$f_{2,j}$
1	;	12	1	B	6
2	=	9	2	A	5
3	IF–THEN	3	3	R	3
4	( ) or group	2	4	0	3
5	/	1	5	G	2
6	−	1	6	GCD	2
7	*	1	$\eta_2 = 6$		$N_2 = 21$
8	GO TO LAST	1			
9	GO TO HERE	1			

$\eta_1 = 9$　　　　　　　　　　$N_1 = 31$

EUCLID'S ALGORITHM IN FORTRAN (*after Zweben*)

```
        IF (A.NE.0) GO TO 1
        GCD = B
        RETURN
1       IF (B.NE.0) GO TO 3
2       GCD = A
        RETURN
3       IG = A/B
        R = A − B * IG
        IF (R.EQ.0) GO TO 2
        A = B
        B = R
        GO TO 3
        END
```

EUCLID'S ALGORITHM IN COMPASS (*after Zweben*)

```
                SA   3    A
                SA   4    B
                NZ        X3, N00001
                BX   6    X4
                SA   6    GCD
            *   EXIT
N00001          NZ        X4, N00002
L00012          BX   6    X3
                SA   6    GCD
            *   EXIT
N00002          FX1       X3/X4
                UX1       B7,X1
                LX1       B7,X1
                PX1       B0,X1
                NX1       B0,X1
                FX1       X4*X1
                FX1       X3−X1
                ZR        X1,L00
                BX3       X4
                BX4       X1
                EQ        N00002
```

Table 6.2
Frequency Counts of Euclid's Algorithm in Fortran (*after Zweben*)

j	Operator	$f_{1,j}$	j	Operand	$f_{2,j}$
1	EOS	10	1	B	6
2	=	6	2	A	5
3	IF	3	3	0	3
4	( ) or Group	3	4	R	3
5	GO TO 3	2	5	GCD	2
6	.NE.	2	6	IG	2
7	GO TO 1	1	$\eta_2 = 6$		$N_2 = 21$
8	GO TO 2	1			
9	–	1			
10	*	1			
11	/	1			
12	.EQ.	1			

$\eta_1 = 12$ $\qquad\qquad\qquad\qquad$ $N_1 = 32$

Table 6.3
Frequency Counts of Euclid's Algorithm in Compass (*after Zweben*)

j	Operator	$f_{1,j}$	j	Operand	$f_{2,j}$
1	EOS	19	1	X1	15
2	ASSIGN	7	2	X4	7
3	TRANSFER	4	3	X3	6
4	CONVERT	2	4	X6	4
5	LOAD OPRND	2	5	0	3
6	SHIFT	2	6	GCD	2
7	STORE OPRND	2	7	B7	2
8	DIVIDE	1	8	A	1
9	SUBFLOAT	1	9	B	1
10	MULTIPLY	1	$\eta_2 = 9$		$N_2 = 41$
11	JP CO N00001	1			
12	JP CO N00002	1			
13	JP CO L00012	1			
14	JP UC N00002	1			

$\eta_1 = 14$ $\qquad\qquad\qquad\qquad$ $N_1 = 45$

In addition to the expressions of the Euclidean algorithm in Algol 58, PL/I, Fortran, and assembly language, we may add two extreme cases, before summarizing the data. First, in potential language

$$GCD\ (\ A\ B\ GCD\ )$$

for which

$$\eta_1 = N_1 = 2$$
$$\eta_2 = N_2 = 3$$

and second, as a "Table-look-up" implementation. For the latter, let us assume that an array of 1000 rows and 1000 columns of previously calculated greatest common divisors is included as the operand "TABLE". The algorithm might then be represented as given below.

EUCLID'S ALGORITHM AS A "TABLE-LOOK-UP" ALGORITHM

```
TABLE:  0, 1,..........
        0, 1,..........
        ............
        ............
GCD := TABLE[ A , B ]
```

Counting parameters above yields the data shown in Table 6.4.

Table 6.4
Frequency Counts for Euclid's Algorithm as a "Table-Look-Up"

j	Operator	$f_{1,j}$	j	Operand	$f_{2,j}$
1	,	1000001	1	TABLE	1000001
2	:	1	2	A	1
3	:=	1	3	B	1
4	[ ]	1	4	GCD	1
$\eta_1 = 4$		$N_1 = 1000004$	$\eta_2 = 4$		$N_2 = 1000004$

Table 6.5
Intelligence Content *I* of Euclid's Algorithm in Various
Languages calculated from Equation (6.2)

Language	η_1	η_2	N_2	N	I
Algol	10	6	21	52	12
PL/I	9	6	21	52	13
Fortran	12	6	21	53	11
Assembly	14	9	41	86	12
Potential	2	3	3	5	12
Table-look-up	4	4	1000004	2000008	12

The observed data for these six versions of the Euclidean algorithm, together with the calculation of the intelligence content *I* from equation (6.2) are shown in Table 6.5.

As expected, as the level employed in implementing this algorithm decreases, the volume required increases proportionately, thereby holding the calculated value of intelligence content to within approximately ±10% of its average.

Results of a similar experiment involving a different algorithm, and from four to nine different programmers per language are given in Table 6.6. Mean values of intelligence content, calculated with equation (6.2) for each of the seven languages were obtained.

Table 6.6
Intelligence Content *I* of Algorithm CACM 13
in Various Languages

Language	I
Algol 58	14
Fortran	15
Cobol	16
Basic	15
Snobol	16
APL	16
PLI/I	16

Again, over some seven languages, the product of level times volume, or intelligence content, remained within ±10% of its average.

Because this property does appear to remain invariant under translation, and only increases as the complexity of a problem increases, it provides a useful language independent measure of the inherent content in a program, or in an English passage. While by definition the intelligence content and the potential volume V^* represent different quantities, they are closely coupled, and may frequently be used interchangeably.

The quantifiable properties I and V^* are potentially quite useful metrics as long as they are used only in a technical sense. They yield a measure of "how much" is expressed, but tell nothing about its importance. As Professor Bohrer has pointed out, software parameters may reveal how well a program has been written, but they do not determine whether the program ever should have been written in the first place.

Chapter 7

Program Purity

In earlier chapters, we saw that the length of a program is related to the size of the vocabulary required for its implementation, and that the product of its volume times its level remains relatively constant when it is translated into another language. The cases for which these relationships were validated by experiment were, however, algorithms selected from a special class. No matter how objectively the selection process was applied, we should note that the algorithms measured were written by experts, probably for publication, and were perhaps modified and improved considerably before they were considered suitable for study or use by other than the original author.

Clearly, any one of these algorithms can be taken and altered in such a way that the observed relationships would be violated, even though the result of executing the algorithm did not change. For example, an implementation that contained an operand named A, and the two operators "add" and "substract," may be modified by adding and then subtracting A one-thousand times, thus increasing N_1 and N_2 without changing η_1 or η_2.

Therefore, it appears that the observed relationships must govern or apply only to algorithmic implementations that are in some sense "pure". Further, by accepting agreement with these relations as a *pseudo*-definition of "pure", a procedure for identifying those constructs that prevent an algorithm from conforming with these relationships can be obtained.

IMPURITY CLASSES

The procedure originally followed in identifying six classes of "impurity" may easily be described. First, a trivial, one-line algorithm was stated as a procedure call. Then this algorithm was implemented in as many ways as came readily to mind. These various ways of possible implementation were intended to include all manner of cumbersome styles, as well as versions that were direct and perhaps "pure". After some 18 versions had been written in this way, each of their values of η_1, η_2, N_1 and N_2 was observed, V and L were calculated, and the product

$L \times V$ ($= V^*$, the potential volume), was obtained. A search was then made for all identifiable "impurities" in the sample. Whenever a construct was identified as an impurity in one version, it was removed from that version and from all other versions in which it was found.

The initial experiment treated as data some 18 versions of the trivial algorithm which squares the sum of the operands P and Q, and places the result in the operand R. Table 7.1 gives the original, unpurified versions of the algorithm.

Complementary Operations—Impurity I

Perhaps the most obvious impurity, on an intuitional basis, consists of the successive application of two complementary operators to the same operand. Optimizing compilers for most programming languages will remove such constructs when they are encountered. It is interesting to note that even in English, for which the double negative creates a positive, translation into Spanish is difficult, because in Spanish, as in many languages, the double negative is not positive, but an emphatic negative.

An examination of Table 7.1 shows that version (5) contains this impurity. In its original form, we have

$$P + Q \rightarrow T, \ T \times T + T - T \rightarrow R$$

for which the expression for $V \times L$ yields

$$V \times L = (N_1 + N_2) \log_2 (\eta_1 + \eta_2) \times \frac{2}{\eta_1} \frac{\eta_2}{N_2}$$

$$= (7 + 8) \log (5 + 4) \times \frac{2}{5} \frac{4}{8} = 9.51$$

Purifying version (5) by removing the complementary operations results in

$$P + Q \rightarrow T, \ T \times T \rightarrow R$$

for which $V \times L$ becomes

$$V \times L = (N_1 + N_2) \log_2 (\eta_1 + \eta_2) \times \frac{2}{\eta_1} \frac{\eta_2}{N_2}$$

$$= (5 + 6) \log_2 (4 + 4) \times \frac{2}{4} \frac{4}{6} = 11.0$$

Table 7.1
Eighteen Unpurified Versions of a Trivial Algorithm

		η_1	η_2	N_1	N_2	V	L	$L \times V$
(1)	SQDSUM(P Q R)	2	3	2	3	12	1.00	11.6
(2)	(P + Q) × (P + Q) → R	4	3	6	5	31	0.30	9.3
(3)	P + Q → R × R → R	3	3	4	5	23	0.40	9.3
(4)	P + Q → T1, P + Q → T2, T1 × T2 → R	4	5	8	9	54	0.28	15.0
(5)	P + Q → T, T × T + T − T → R	5	4	7	8	48	0.20	9.5
(6)	SUM(P Q T), SQR(T R)	4	4	5	5	30	0.40	12.0
(7)	P × (P + Q) + Q × (P + Q) → R	4	3	8	7	42	0.21	9.1
(8)	P + Q → R, R × R → R	4	3	5	6	31	0.25	7.7
(9)	P + Q → T1, T1 ↑ 2 → R	4	5	5	6	35	0.42	14.5
(10)	P + Q → T, T × T + T − T + T − T → R	5	4	9	10	60	0.16	9.6
(11)	(P + Q) ↑ 2 → R	4	4	4	4	24	0.50	12.0
(12)	P × P + P × Q + P × Q + Q × Q → R	3	3	8	9	44	0.22	9.8
(13)	SUM(P Q R), SQR(R R)	4	3	5	5	28	0.30	8.4
(14)	P → T1, Q → T2, T1 + T2 → T3, T3 × T3 → R	4	6	9	10	63	0.30	19.0
(15)	LDAP ADDQ STOT MPYT STOR	4	4	5	5	30	0.40	12.0
(16)	P ↑ 2 + Q ↑ 2 + 2 × P × Q → R	4	4	7	8	45	0.25	11.2
(17)	P + Q → T, T × T → R	4	4	5	6	33	0.33	11.0
(18)	P × P + 2 × P × Q + Q × Q → R	3	4	7	8	42	0.33	14.0

which is much closer to the potential volume value of 11.6 than the un-purified version is. Examination of Table 7.1 shows that version (10) also contains this impurity.

Ambiguous Operands—Impurity II

The use of a given operand name to refer to different things at different places in a program occurs whenever an earlier use of a name is no longer needed and a later use is initiated. For a computer language that lacks the capability to equivalence two operand names, this usage may actually save storage. Nonetheless, ambiguous uses of operand names tend to reduce comprehensibility of a program, just as, in English, the use of terms whose meaning must be obtained from context increases the diffi-culty of understanding.

Version (8) is an example of such usage, inasmuch as the operand R is first used to represent a sum, and then later a square. In its original form, version (8) or

$$P + Q \to R, \, R \times R \to R$$

yields

$$V \times L = (N_1 + N_2) \log_2(\eta_1 + \eta_2) \times \frac{2}{\eta_1} \frac{\eta_2}{N_2}$$

$$= (5 + 6) \log_2(4 + 3) \times \frac{2}{4} \times \frac{3}{6} = 7.7$$

Purifying version (8) by removing the ambiguous usage of R yields

$$P + Q \to T, \, T \times T \to R$$

which gives $V \times L$ as

$$V \times L = (5 + 6) \log_2(4 + 4) \times \frac{2}{4} \frac{4}{6} = 11.0$$

Here again, the purified value 11.0 is closer to the theoretical value 11.6 than the version containing the ambiguous usage. Versions (3) and (13) in Table 7.1 also contain this impurity.

Synonomous Operands—Impurity III

The complement of ambiguity in naming operands is the use of two different names for the same thing. If two or more variables are used in such a way that their values must always be identical, then the synonymous operand impurity is present. Version (4), in its original form, contains this impurity, since T1 and T2 must be identical.

$$P + Q \rightarrow T1, \; P + Q \rightarrow T2, \; T1 \times T2 \rightarrow R$$

yields, for $V \times L$

$$V \times L = (N_1 + N_2) \log_2 (\eta_1 + \eta_2) \times \frac{2}{\eta_1} \frac{\eta_2}{N_2}$$

$$= (8 + 9) \log_2 (4 + 5) \times \frac{2}{4} \frac{5}{8} = 15.0$$

Purification of version (4) by removing the synonymous operand T2 gives

$$P + Q \rightarrow T1, \; T1 \times T1 \rightarrow R$$

which yields $V \times L$ as

$$V \times L = (5 + 6) \log_2 (4 + 4) \times \frac{2}{4} \frac{4}{6} = 11.0$$

in addition to version (4), version (14) of Table 7.1 contains an instance of synonymous operand usage.

Common Subexpressions—Impurity IV

Whenever a specific combination of terms must be used more than once, it is customary to assign a new name to that combination, and then to use the new name in subsequent references. Whenever this practice is not followed, a program contains common subexpressions. While the optimization phase of a compiler may be able to eliminate common subexpressions, if it does not, then unneeded calculations are performed.

In Table 7.1, version (2) given below contains two instances of the expression $(P + Q)$

$$(P + Q) \times (P + Q) \rightarrow R$$

which gives, for $L \times V$

$$L \times V = (N_1 + N_2) \log_2 (\eta_1 + \eta_2) \times \frac{2}{\eta_1} \frac{\eta_2}{N_2}$$

$$= (6 + 5) \log_2 (4 + 3) \times \frac{2}{4} \frac{3}{5} = 9.3$$

Purifying version (2) by eliminating the common subexpression gives

$$P + Q \rightarrow T, \; T \times T \rightarrow R$$

so that $V \times L$ becomes

$$V \times L = (5 + 6) \log_2 (4 + 4) \times \frac{2}{4} \times \frac{4}{6} = 11.0$$

In addition to version (2), versions (7) and (12) also contain this common subexpression impurity.

Unwarranted Assignment—Impurity V

In a sense the opposite of the common subexpression impurity is the case in which a combination of terms is assigned a unique name, but then used only once. The new name serves no useful purpose, since the subexpression is not common to any other part of the program. In Table 7.1, the only version of the algorithm containing an unwarranted assignment, in this case to T1, is version (9).

$$P + Q \rightarrow T1, \; T1 \uparrow 2 \rightarrow R$$

for which $V \times L$ is given by

$$V \times L = (N_1 + N_2) \log_2 (\eta_1 + \eta_2) \times \frac{2}{\eta_1} \frac{\eta_2}{N_2}$$

$$= (5 + 6) \log_2 (4 + 5) \times \frac{2}{4} \frac{5}{6} = 14.5$$

Purifying version (9) by removing the unwarranted assignment to T1 yields

$$(P + Q) \uparrow 2 \rightarrow R$$

which gives

$$V \times L = (4 + 4) \log_2 (4 + 4) \times \frac{2}{4} \frac{4}{4} = 12.0$$

Unfactored Expressions—Impurity VI

While it is intuitively clear that an expression that can be factored is easier to comprehend after factoring, the sixth impurity class that deals with this case is different from the previous five impurity classes inasmuch as no mechanical method of removing this impurity is known. On the other hand, its occurrence in actual programs is apparently quite rare. In Table 7.1, its only instance is in version (18), or

$$P \times P + 2 \times P \times Q + Q \times Q \to R$$

which gives, for $V \times L$

$$V \times L = (N_1 + N_2) \log_2(\eta_1 + \eta_2) \times \frac{2}{\eta_1} \frac{\eta_2}{N_2}$$

$$= (7 + 8) \log_2(3 + 4) \times \frac{2}{3} \times \frac{4}{8} = 14.0$$

Table 7.2
**Values of $V \times L$ Before and After Removing
All Six Impurities**

Version[a]	Original $V \times L$	Impurity Removed	Purified $V \times L$
(1)	11.6	none	11.6
(2)	9.3	IV	11.0
(3)	9.3	II	13.4
(4)	15.0	III	11.0
(5)	9.5	I	11.0
(6)	12.0	none	12.0
(7)	9.1	IV	12.0
(8)	7.7	II	11.0
(9)	14.5	V	12.0
(10)	9.6	I	11.0
(11)	12.0	none	12.0
(12)	9.8	IV	11.4
(13)	8.4	II	12.0
(14)	19.0	III	11.0
(15)	12.0	none	12.0
(16)	11.2	none	11.2
(17)	11.0	none	11.0
(18)	14.0	VI	12.0

[a]From Table 7.1.

Purifying version (18) by factoring it gives

$$(P + Q) \uparrow 2 \rightarrow R$$

which yields

$$V \times L = (4\,4 + 4)\log_2(4 + 4) \times \frac{2\,4}{4\,4} = 12.0$$

where again, purification produces an improvement in the agreement between the product $V \times L$ and V^*.

Extending the purification process to all of the versions in Table 7.1 yields the results summarized in Table 7.2.

In Table 7.2, we note that versions (1), (6), (11), (15), (16), and (17), although all different, contain none of the six impurities defined above, and that their values of $V \times L$ fall into the range from 11.0 to 12.0.

SIGNIFICANCE OF IMPURITIES

Perhaps it appears from the way in which the six impurity classes have been identified and described that an attempt is being made to justify the view that each impurity is an instance of poor programming practice. But even if these impurities are precisely that, the mere fact that their removal improves the agreement between V^* and $V \times L$ gives absolutely no evidence that they are instances of poor programming practice.

In other words, it is well known that the scientific approach cannot be used as evidence that any reasonable argument is correct, solely because it is reasonable. Instead, validation must depend on experimental evidence. Consequently, all that can be stated in regard to the "goodness" or "badness" of impurities is that programs written by first-semester programming students usually contain fairly large numbers of impurities, while programs published in the computing literature contain virtually none of them. Further, as reported by Zislis [38], semantic partitioning cannot be achieved without the removal of several impurity classes.

Chapter 8

Programming Effort

If we restrict the concept of programming effort to be the mental activity required to reduce a preconceived algorithm to an actual implementation in a language in which the implementor (writer) is fluent, then the metrics and concepts introduced in the previous chapters provide both a useful insight into the programming process, and a frame of reference for its quantification.

The simple relationship between these metrics and the effort required by a programmer may be obtained by following the six rather straightforward steps, as outlined below.

DERIVATION OF THE EFFORT EQUATION

STEP (1)

Assume, as before, that any implementation of any algorithm consists of N selections from a vocabulary of η elements.

STEP (2)

Further, assume that each and every selection from the vocabulary η must be made on a nonrandom basis. Research on sorting has shown that, with the possible exception of hash coding, the most efficient possible search of an ordered list is a binary search. In a binary search, a list is repetitively halved until the desired element is found, with the result that the number of comparisons required is equal to the binary logarithm of the number of elements in the list. An efficient process, equivalent to a binary search, therefore requires $\log_2 \eta$ comparisons for selection of each element.

STEP (3)

From steps (1) and (2), it follows that a program is generated by making $N \times \log_2 \eta$ mental comparisons.

STEP (4)

Since the program volume V is defined as

$$V = N \log_2 \eta \qquad (8.1)$$

it follows from step (3) that the volume is a count of the number of mental comparisons required to generate a program.

STEP (5)

Each mental comparison requires a number of elementary mental discriminations, where this number is a measure of the difficulty of the task. From the results of Chapter 5, it follows that program level L is the reciprocal of program difficulty.

STEP (6)

Since the volume V is a count of the mental comparisons, and the reciprocal of program level, or $1/L$, is a measure of the average number of elementary mental discriminations required for each mental comparison, it follows that the *total number of elementary mental discriminations* E required to generate a given program should be given by

$$E = \frac{V}{L} \qquad (8.2)$$

A further implication of the effort equation can be shown by recalling equation (5.1)

$$L = \frac{V*}{V}$$

and substituting in equation (8.2), giving

$$E = \frac{V^2}{V*} \qquad (8.3)$$

Equation (8.3) indicates that the mental effort required to implement any algorithm with a given potential volume should vary with the square of its volume in any language, rather than linearly. As will be investigated in detail in Chapter 12, equation (8.3) further implies that, since "the square of the sum is greater than the sum of the squares", properly designed modularization can definitely reduce programming effort for partitionable programs.

Now it will be somewhat more straightforward to design an experiment to test the effort equation, equation (8.2), if that relationship is first extended from a simple count of elementary mental discriminations to a measure of time.

DISCRIMINATIONS PER UNIT TIME

Let us consider a concept developed by John Stroud, a psychologist, in "The Fine Structure of Psychological Time". Stroud defined a "moment" as the time required by the human brain to perform the most elementary discrimination. He reported that, for all waking, conscious time, these "moments" occurred at a rate of "from five to twenty or a little less" per second. While Stroud was seeking the internal processing rate of the brain, as distinct from the input/output rate, it is reassuring to note that his figures include within their range the number of frames per second which a motion picture must have to appear as a continuous picture rather than as single frames. Denoting Stroud's "moments" per second by S, we have

$$5 \leq S \leq 20 \text{ per second}$$

Hereafter, S is referred to as the Stroud number.

Now it is true, of course, that anyone engaged in implementing an algorithm may, depending on his degree of concentration, be devoting some fraction of his available mental discriminations to extraneous subjects. In the terminology of computers, if he is "time-sharing", S represents only an upper limit. On the other hand, if a programmer enforces the equivalent of the computer operation, "inhibit all interrupts," and concentrates on the programming task alone, then the actual value of S is applicable.

This requirement for mental concentration suggests that careful attention to this point must be provided for in all work on experimental validation.

To convert equation (8.2), which has the dimensions of both binary digits and of discriminations, to units of time, we merely divide both sides by discriminations per unit time, giving

$$\hat{T} = \frac{E}{S} = \frac{V}{SL} = \frac{V^2}{SV^*} \qquad (8.4)$$

where the hat has been placed over the time T to indicate that equation (8.4) yields an estimated, rather than an observed value of programming time.

Equation (8.4) may be expressed in terms of the basic parameters by substituting for V from equation (3.1), and for L from equation (5.5), giving

$$\hat{T} = \frac{\eta_1 N_2 N \log_2 \eta}{2S\eta_2} \qquad (8.5)$$

In the preceding derivation, it is tacitly assumed that all programs are pure, in the sense that they contain none of the impurity classes discussed in Chapter 7. While this assumption may be valid for published programs, and reasonably close for others, it is not necessary to make it. Instead, this assumption is removed, at least to a first approximation, by substituting $\hat{N}$ for N in equation (8.5). Performing this substitution, where $\hat{N}$ is given by the length equation (2.7), yields

$$\hat{T} = \frac{\eta_1 N_2 (\eta_1 \log_2 \eta_1 + \eta_2 \log_2 \eta_2) \log_2 \eta}{2\eta_2 S} \qquad (8.6)$$

where, except for the Stroud number S, all of the parameters on the right are directly measurable for any implementation of any algorithm.

EXPERIMENTAL VALIDATION OF THE PROGRAMMING TIME RELATIONSHIP

Equation (8.6) is called the *time equation*. Just as any other useful relationship in the natural sciences, it must be subjected to experimental verification. Most published data on programming rates contain program sizes and man-hours, but neither the programs themselves, nor the basic software parameters. Neither the degree of concentration, nor the measure of difficulty is known. For very large programs, this situation must be accepted, and later in this chapter we consider methods of approximating the time equation for that situation. For smaller programming tasks, however, this limitation does not apply. The results of two separate series of experiments designed specifically to test equation (8.6) have

Table 8.1
Raw Data From Programming Experiment

CACM No.	(14)	(14)	(14)	(14)	(16)	(16)	(16)	(16)
Iteration i	0	1	2	3	0	1	2	3
Language	P	F	A	P	F	A	P	F
Time (minutes)	33	15	25	7	135	77	44	31
η_1	15	16	20	15	20	20	15	20
η_2	17	20	21	17	35	21	21	38
N_1	64	48	70	63	223	264	245	200
N_2	51	55	68	49	303	241	205	272

CACM No.	(17)	(17)	(17)	(17)	(19)	(19)	(19)	(19)
Iteration i	0	1	2	3	0	1	2	3
Language	A	P	F	A	P	A	F	P
Time (minutes)	33	10	11	9	7	10	9	6
η_1	15	8	10	15	10	14	11	13
η_2	15	12	16	15	6	9	11	8
N_1	78	84	73	94	25	31	22	29
N_2	81	70	78	95	19	32	29	23

CACM No.	(20)	(20)	(20)	(20)	(21)	(21)	(21)	(21)
Iteration i	0	1	2	3	0	1	2	3
Language	P	A	F	P	A	P	F	A
Time (minutes)	12	14	6	5	43	30	39	22
η_1	14	12	11	11	23	20	20	23
η_2	19	19	18	16	25	27	43	27
N_1	59	43	49	54	106	142	109	116
N_2	38	37	35	32	97	114	153	115

CACM No.	(23)	(23)	(23)	(23)	(24)	(24)	(24)	(24)
Iteration i	0	1	2	3	0	1	2	3
Language	A	F	P	A	A	P	F	A
Time (minutes)	21	13	13	19	16	8	6	8
η_1	17	8	8	15	15	8	7	14
η_2	13	18	12	16	14	9	14	12
N_1	50	32	48	51	81	84	66	97
N_2	50	50	38	60	82	74	77	97

(Table continues on next page.)

CACM No.	(25)	(25)	(25)	(25)	(29)	(29)	(29)	(29)
Iteration i	0	1	2	3	0	1	2	3
Language	A	F	P	A	P	F	A	P
Time (minutes)	62	45	20	29	25	35	16	9
η_1	26	24	18	22	7	8	15	8
η_2	34	43	35	41	11	18	17	12
N_1	179	122	162	156	72	64	64	75
N_2	163	138	122	155	67	89	65	79

CACM No.	(31)	(31)	(31)	(31)	(33)	(33)	(33)	(33)
Iteration i	0	1	2	3	0	1	2	3
Language	F	A	P	F	F	P	A	F
Time (minutes)	20	11	7	7	4	3	3	3
η_1	17	14	12	15	6	8	9	6
η_2	25	25	19	24	8	3	5	8
N_1	53	59	67	50	9	12	11	10
N_2	54	63	44	51	15	6	11	17

NOTE. P stands for PL/I; F for Fortran; A for APL.

been published, and these are described first, before considering large programming tasks.

PROGRAMMING TIME EXPERIMENT—SERIES (1)

A computer scientist, fluent in three languages: PL/I, Fortran, and APL, accepted the following assignment, to be performed as a part-time activity over a period of five months:

(1) Select a dozen algorithms published in Algol, in areas familiar to him, from the *Communications of the Association for Computing Machinery*.

(2) From the Comments and Introductory Statements accompanying the published algorithms, and, if needed, the Algol versions themselves, prepare rough specifications for those twelve algorithms.

(3) Using a random process, select an initial implementation language from the set: PL/I, Fortran, and APL separately for each of the dozen algorithms.

(4) Maintaining a high degree of mental concentration, and accurate records of time required for coding and desk checking, program each of the algorithms from the specifications in the selected language.

(5) Again at random, select a second implementation language for each algorithm.

(6) Repeat step (4) with the second language.

(7) Repeat step (4) with the remaining (third) language.

(8) In order to obtain information on the learning effect of repetition, repeat step (4) with the initial language.

(9) After all of the 48 implementations have been completed, obtain counts of η_1, η_2, N_1, and N_2 for each.

The raw data from this experiment are summarized in Table 8.1.

Analysis of the effect of learning, or increased familiarity with the twelve algorithms over the five-month period of the experiment, suggests that this factor is highly significant only when an algorithm was repeated in the same language, or implementation (4).

Using a Stroud number of 18 per second, or 1080 per minute, the observed values of η_1, η_2, and N_2 from Table 8.1 were then used to calculate $\hat{T}$ from equation (8.6) for the first three implementations of each algorithm. Table 8.2 gives these values of $\hat{T}$ as compared with the observed programming times T in minutes.

From Table 8.2 it can be seen that the total programming time for the complete series was 14 hours and 41 minutes, compared with a total of 15 hours and 27 minutes calculated from equation (8.6). While the mean values obtained from the theory will change if a different value of the Stroud number is used, this has no effect on the coefficients of correlation. Consequently, the fact that all three Pearsonian coefficients of correlation between theory and observation are greater then 0.9 is of considerably greater importance than the agreement of the mean values.

A further test of the power of the theory can be obtained from the same experimental series. Since Ida Rhodes of the Bureau of Standards noted, more than 20 years ago, that coding time approximated four instructions per man-hour, the field has been aware that longer programs usually, *but not always*, take longer to program than short ones. Now if the theory merely agrees with the general trend that longer programs take longer to write, it would still be of value inasmuch as it provides actual time units. On the other hand, if it also differentiates between

Table 8.2
Observed and Theoretical Programming Times for Experimental Series (1)

CACM Number	Implementation						Mean	
	First		Second		Third			
	T	$\hat{T}$	T	$\hat{T}$	T	$\hat{T}$	T	$\hat{T}$
(14)	33	13	15	16	25	29	24	19
(16)	135	123	77	102	44	53	85	93
(17)	33	22	10	6	11	10	18	13
(19)	7	3	10	9	9	5	9	6
(20)	12	9	14	7	6	5	11	7
(21)	43	51	30	47	39	63	37	54
(23)	21	17	13	5	13	3	16	8
(24)	16	22	8	7	6	6	10	12
(25)	62	101	45	74	20	42	42	72
(29)	25	5	35	9	16	17	25	10
(31)	20	17	11	15	7	8	13	13
(33)	4	1	3	1	3	1	3	1
Sums	411	384	271	298	199	242	293	309
Means	34	32	23	25	17	20	24	26
Coefficient of correlation	0.92		0.92		0.94		0.94	

two programs of the same length on the basis of their difficulty, then a much more basic or fundamental property is implied. In order to test this hypothesis, the number of statements in the original published versions of each of the 12 algorithms were counted. The results are then compared with the three-language averages from Table 8.2. The analysis is given in Table 8.3, where the data are arranged in order of increasing values of measured programming times.

For this series of experiments, at least, it appears from Table 8.3 that the theory explains about three-fourths of the variance that remains after the correlation with program length, as measured by number of statements, is accounted for. Consequently, the hypothesis that equation (8.6) properly combines the two major factors, difficulty and amount, is not invalidated by this series of experiments.

Table 8.3
Comparison of Theory vs Length as Estimates of Programming Times
for Experimental Series (1)

CACM No.	Number of statements	Observed Time (minutes)	Theoretical Time (minutes)
(33)	1	3	1
(19)	5	9	6
(24)	8	10	12
(20)	6	11	7
(31)	15	13	13
(23)	7	16	8
(17)	9	18	13
(14)	22	24	19
(29)	14	25	10
(21)	12	37	54
(25)	57	42	72
(16)	35	85	93
Correlation coefficient with T observed	0.70	1.00	0.94

PROGRAMMING TIME EXPERIMENT—SERIES (2)

Another series of experiments has also been reported, by a second computer scientist. This series was designed to be more readily reproduced than the first, and was performed entirely in Fortran with no repetitions. The experimental procedure was the following.

Eleven problem statements were selected from computer textbooks. In selecting candidates for the experiment, problems sought were those stated in a nonprocedural form. Further, the problem statement had to be complete. That is, in the course of solving a particular problem, specific laws of physics, mathematics, etc., would not have to be derived. The eleven problems selected cover a wide range of topics including character manipulation, list processing, simulation experiments and mathematical analysis. The source of each problem statement is cited in Table 8.4.

On each of eleven days the experimenter implemented one of these test algorithms. In order to maintain a high degree of concentration all work was conducted in a quiet room, free from distractions, during the same period of the day. The time required to implement the problem completely was obtained. This total time included the number of minutes spent reading the statement of the problem, preparing flowcharts and writing preliminary versions of the code, writing the final version of the code, desk checking, and the time spent working to correct errors in the program. Time to keypunch was not included. In the course of solving a problem the correctness of the implementation was checked by executing a sufficiently complex test case for which a correct answer was known. In some cases the solution to a problem was written as a subroutine and testing required that a main routine be written. In such a case only the preparation of the subroutine was considered for the experiment. In addition, several implementations made use of subroutines previously written.

After all programs were completed, a careful count was made to determine values of η_1, η_2, N_1, and N_2. In obtaining these values all read, write, declarative statements and comments were ignored. The results are shown in Table 8.4. In the problem source column, the designator "K" refers to Knuth's *The Art of Computer Programming,* Volume 1,

Table 8.4
Raw Data from Programming Experiment—Series (2)

Program No.	Program Specifications			Software Parameters				Implementation (minutes)
	Ref.	Page	Problem	η_1	η_2	N_1	N_2	
G1	K	158	21	15	11	59	51	19
G2	K	159	23	20	24	231	197	92
G3	K	196	7	16	12	64	49	16
G4	K	377	17	19	21	131	113	39
G5	K	158	22	7	10	38	35	21
G6	K	154	10	9	14	69	62	30
G7	M	32	3.2.21	12	8	30	23	5
G8	M	32	3.2.23	19	15	73	55	24
G9	M	88	8.3.2	22	32	124	104	43
G10	M	89	8.3.4	25	34	261	222	91
G11	M	27	3.2.4	14	10	29	21	5

NOTE. K stands for Knuth; M for Maurer and Williams.

Table 8.5
Comparison of Theory vs Statement Counts as Estimates
of Programming Times for Experimental Series (2)

Program No.	Statement Count	Programming Time (minutes)	
		T (observed)	T (from eq. (8.6))
G7	7	5	5
G11	8	5	5
G5	11	21	2
G6	15	30	7
G3	18	16	16
G1	18	19	15
G8	18	24	23
G4	32	39	44
G2	36	92	82
G9	38	43	49
G10	59	91	129
Sum	260	385	377
Mean	24	35	34
Coefficient of correlation with T observed	0.89	1.00	0.93

and the designator "M" refers to Maurer and Williams' *A Collection of Programming Problems and Techniques.*

Applying equation (8.6) to the data in Table 8.4, again taking a Stroud number of 18 per second, gives the values of $\hat{T}$ in Table 8.5. In addition to the observed and calculated programming times, a count of the number of Fortran statements in the final programs was made, and entered in the table.

Here again, the mean value predicted by the timing equation is in general agreement with the observed average time, and the coefficient of correlation between individual values is above 0.9. For series (2), the statement count, while not as good a predictor as the timing equation, is better than it was for series (1). Perhaps this should have been expected, because series (2) involves only one implementation language, rather than the three of series (1).

TIMING EQUATION APPROXIMATIONS
WHEN ONLY LENGTH IS KNOWN

It was found in the previous sections that the timing equation possesses two important advantages when compared with a simple correlation between number of statements and programming time. First, it appears to account for variations in the difficulty of programs. Second, in conjunction with the Stroud number, it provides estimates in units of elapsed time.

Now if data on programming times versus program length are available, but the basic metrics, η_1, η_2, N_1, and N_2 cannot be measured, the first advantage is unavailable, but it may still be possible to obtain the second. One approach to this problem appears to be especially applicable to machine language programs. If we define P as the *number of actual machine instructions* in a program, where memory reserved for data is not included, then there must be a close relationship between P and program length N. For most early computers, each instruction contained an operation code, an operand or operand address, and the option of including an indexing operation with a specifiable index. Consequently, when an instruction without indexing occurs, it contributes one to N_1 and one to N_2, or a total of two to N. When an indexing instruction occurs, it must contribute two to N_1 and two to N_2, for a total of four to N. The relation is therefore bounded by

$$2P \leq N \leq 4P \qquad (8.7)$$

A precise relationship could be obtained if the frequency of indexing were known. A reasonable estimate of this frequency may be taken from Knuth's statistical study of a quarter of a million Fortran statements. In that study, Knuth reported that 79% of operands were variables, and that 42% of variables were indexed. These figures yield the approximation

$$N = 2(1 + 0.79 \times 0.42)P = 2(1 + 0.33)P \qquad (8.8)$$

or

$$N = \frac{8}{3}P \qquad (8.9)$$

which provides a close approximation to length from the number of machine language instructions.

Now, starting with the timing equation (8.6), and making the simplifying assumptions that

$$\eta_1 = \eta_2 = \tfrac{1}{2}\eta \tag{8.10}$$

and

$$N_1 = N_2 = \tfrac{1}{2}N = \tfrac{1}{2}\hat{N} \tag{8.11}$$

yields

$$\hat{T} = \frac{N^2 \log_2 \eta}{4S} \tag{8.12}$$

where η may be obtained from N from the relation

$$N = \eta \log_2 (\eta/2) \tag{8.13}$$

Because of the simplifying assumptions used in obtaining equation (8.12), especially that of equation (8.10), it cannot be expected to differentiate between programs on the basis of complexity. Since η varies with N, it follows that equation (8.12) predicts that effort for machine language programs increases slightly more rapidly than the square of the number of instructions.

APPROXIMATION VALIDATION
FOR MACHINE LANGUAGE PROGRAMMING

A set of data on machine language programmer productivity from a paper presented by the author at a conference in 1961 are shown in Table 8.6. They have the advantage that they were obtained during an era and from a group, in which a high degree of mental concentration could be assumed.

While the small sample size of Table 8.6 suggests that the extremely high coefficients of correlation should not be accepted at face value, the variations among them are of considerable interest. First, it should be noted that N is related linearly to P, and as a consequence the coefficients of correlation between T and N and between T and P must be equal. Similarly, since T is obtained from E by dividing by the Stroud number, $S = 18$ mental discriminations per second, those two coefficients must also be equal. The interesting point is that for observed programming times ranging from approximately half of a day to nearly three-fourths of a man-year, the approximation given by equation (8.12) yields a higher correlation than length alone.

Table 8.6

Machine Language Programming Times Observed, and as Predicted on the Basis of Length Alone [*Equation* (8.12)]

No.	Observed Time T(hours)	Number of Instructions P	From Eq. (8.9) N	From Eq. (8.13) η	Elementary Discriminations E(millions)	Predicted Time T(hours)
(1)	4.9	120	320	64	0.154	2.4
(2)	8.8	230	613	107	0.634	9.8
(3)	118	590	1573	230	4.86	75.0
(4)	40	620	1653	239	5.40	83.0
(5)	80	710	1893	268	7.23	112.0
(6)	358	1000	2667	357	15.1	233.0
(7)	1430	2000	5333	641	66.3	1023.0
Correlation		0.949	0.949	0.956	0.997	0.997

Another machine language data point, taken from the same era, can be obtained from John Backus' report upon the completion of the first Fortran compiler in 1957. According to the paper he presented to the Western Joint Computer Conference that year, a programming effort of 18 man-years produced the six modules whose number of instructions are shown in Table 8.7. Times for the individual modules were not given, but if we estimate by letting one man-year equal 50 weeks of 40 man-hours each, then the total was 36,000 man-hours. Using the same notation and equations used in Table 8.6, we have the results given in Table 8.7.

While the data presented in this chapter tend to confirm the simple hypothesis used to derive both the timing equation (8.6) and the approximation to it for machine language programming, equation (8.12), at this point that hypothesis is merely explanatory, rather than truly predictive. This is because it is not until after an algorithm has been implemented that observations of η_1, η_2, N_1, and N_2 are available. This important restriction can be removed by employing the relationships between these forgoing metrics and two properties, one invariant over algorithms, and one invariant over a specified language. The first of these, V^*, or η_2^* obtained from it, was discussed in Chapter 3. The second, language

Table 8.7
Estimation of Original Fortran Compiler Implementation Time

Section No.	Instructions P	Length N	η	Discriminations E(millions)	Estimated Time T(hours)
(1)	5,500	14,700	1540	570	8,800
(2)	6,000	16,000	1650	685	10,600
(3)	2,500	6,600	770	104	1,600
(4)	3,000	8,000	908	157	2,400
(5)	5,000	13,300	1404	464	7,200
(6)	2,000	5,300	636	65	1,000

Total estimated time (man-hours)	31,600	
Total observed time (man-hours)	36,000	
Difference (%)		12.2

level λ, is treated in Chapter 9, and further their combined use for prediction is discussed in Chapter 10.

In the meantime, it might be well to consider a few of the implications that appear to follow from the effort hypothesis. First, the hypothesis was obtained by assuming the following three conditions:

(1) Availability of a complete problem statement.
(2) Fluency in the language employed.
(3) Complete concentration.

If any of these stated conditions is absent, and this is often the case, then the hypothesis as developed merely provides a lower limit. In fact, it has been suggested that by providing assurance for conditions (1) and (3), the hypothesis might serve as a test of fluency. Nevertheless, the really interesting condition is the first one, involving a complete problem statement. This results from the fact that whether or not a problem statement is complete depends not only on the author who writes the statement, but on the programmer who reads it. Even though a statement, written at a given level in English, is complete for one group of programmers, another group less familiar with that subject area might find it to be presented at too high a level, hence not complete.

Chapter 9

Language Level

The program level L and the program volume V exhibit a useful relationship as discussed in Chapter 5. For any given algorithm that is translated from one implementation language to another, as the volume increases, the level decreases proportionately. Consequently, the product of L time V equals the potential volume V^* for any one algorithm.

On the other hand, when the implementation language is held constant, and the algorithm itself is allowed to vary, there is a different, but similar relationship to be observed. For this case, as the potential volume V^* increases, the program level L decreases proportionately. Consequently, the product L times V^* remains constant for any one language. This product, the *language level,* is denoted by lambda, or λ, so that

$$\lambda = LV^* \tag{9.1}$$

The significance of what is involved in equation (9.1) is explored in detail in a later section. First, however, we must establish experimentally that the relationship agrees with observations.

VALIDATION OF THE LANGUAGE RELATIONSHIP

Equation (9.1) may be tested in the following way. Substituting the product $L \times V$ for V^* in equation (9.1) gives

$$\lambda = L(L \times V) = L^2V \tag{9.2}$$

Now if the exponent 2 is replaced by an arbitrary exponent, say b, then it is possible, by using data from a range of different algorithms, to solve for b. If the result is sufficiently close to $b = 2$, then equation (9.2) may be accepted, and with it, equation (9.1). Starting, then, with

$$\lambda = L^bV \tag{9.3}$$

and taking natural logarithms of both sides gives

$$\ln \eta = \ln (L^bV) \tag{9.4}$$

or

$$\ln \lambda = \ln L^b + \ln V \tag{9.5}$$

or

$$\ln \lambda = b \ln L + \ln V \tag{9.6}$$

Now if, temporarily, we set

$$a = \ln \lambda \tag{9.7}$$

$$X = \ln V \tag{9.8}$$

and

$$Y = -\ln L \tag{9.9}$$

then equation (9.6) can be expressed as

$$X = a + bY \tag{9.10}$$

By putting equation (9.3) in this form, it is easy to notice that b is merely the slope of the line of regression of X on Y. Consequently, an estimate of b can be obtained from any set of data by using a simple statistical technique.

Seven independent samples are available, covering the languages Algol 58, PL/I, Fortran, and the machine language Compass. The data are given in Table 9.1. In order to minimize the effect of the tendency of samples to cluster around their mean volumes, all samples have been partioned into class intervals such that

$$2^i \leqslant V < 2^{i+1} \tag{9.11}$$

The number of programs contributing to the mean for each class interval is also entered, as n in Table 9.1. Values of the coefficient of correlation r for each language sample are given, as well as the statistical estimate of the exponent b. Values of b have been obtained from the relation

$$b = \frac{\Sigma XY - N \bar{X} \bar{Y}}{\Sigma Y^2 - N \bar{Y}^2} \tag{9.12}$$

where N is the number of class intervals in a given sample.

From the seven values of the coefficient of correlation r between the logarithm of volume and $1/L$, it is apparent that these two quantities are as closely coupled as equation (9.2) suggests.

The individual estimates of b, together with the total number of programs n from which each was obtained, are summarized in Table 9.2.

Table 9.1
Volume vs Program Level Data—Language and Sample Source

i	Algol 58 (after Halstead)			Algol 58 (after Bulut)			PL/I (after Elshoff)			Restr. PL/I (after Elshoff)			Fortran (after Bohrer)			Fortran (after Bulut)			Compass (after Bulut)		
	n	X	Y	n	X	Y	n	X	Y	n	X	Y	n	X	Y	n	X	Y	n	X	Y
7	5	5.43	2.91	4	5.40	2.72							1	5.17	3.14	2	5.42	2.82	1	5.32	3.4
8	1	6.13	3.12	3	6.03	3.01										6	5.87	3.01	5	5.88	3.5
9	4	6.57	3.32	3	6.44	3.34				2	6.50	2.68	4	6.62	3.41	4	6.47	3.37	1	6.55	3.7
10							3	7.33	3.59	5	7.13	3.21	6	7.12	3.72						
11	2	7.70	3.76	2	7.67	3.85	2	8.25	3.66	4	7.89	3.92	2	7.61	4.20	2	7.78	4.08			
12							6	8.64	3.90	11	8.73	4.04									
13							8	9.29	4.06	15	9.42	4.36									
14							5	10.24	4.63	30	10.08	4.89									
15							8	10.87	4.65	28	10.67	5.20									
16							2	12.48	5.35	19	11.41	5.74									
17										6	12.08	6.11									
r	0.997			0.994			0.947			0.993			0.918			0.999			0.988		
b	2.62			1.96			2.57			1.68			2.13			1.84			3.40		

Table 9.2
Estimating Value of Exponent b
of Equation (9.3) from 212 Programs of Table 9.1

Language	Sample	n	b
Algol 58	Halstead	12	2.62
Algol 58	Bulut	12	1.96
PL/I	Elshoff	34	2.57
PL/I (Restr.)	Elshoff	120	1.68
Fortran	Bohrer	13	2.13
Fortran	Bulut	14	1.84
Compass	Bulut	7	3.40
Weighted Mean			1.987

Weighting each estimate of b by the number of programs in its sample, and averaging, provides a reasonable estimate of its value.

While the variance is rather large, the fact that the largest sample yet available yields an estimate of 1.987 for b may be taken as experimental support for $b = 2$ in equation (9.3). From this it follows that both equations (9.2) and (9.1) agree with experimental evidence.

EFFECT OF BLOCK SIZE β ON LANGUAGE LEVEL λ

Although the experimental approach of the previous section may be considered adequate to establish the relation for the language level, two rather different experiments lend support in other ways. The first of these is described in this section.

Intuitively, it has long been recognized that the larger the block size, the higher the level, although this has usually been expressed as a caution against liberal use of the GO TO statement.

If we define ν as the count of *transfers,* both conditional and unconditional, in a program, and β as the average *block size,* then

$$\beta = \frac{N}{\nu + 1} \qquad (9.13)$$

and it would be expected that, if the widely held opinion is correct, there should be a positive correlation between β and λ for any given language.

This can be demonstrated on a set of 14 Fortran programs, published with their software metrics by Zweben. Their values of ν were obtained by counting each occurrence of any of the three statements

   (1)   GO TO LABEL
   (2)   IF (   ) EXPRESSION
   (3)   IF (   ) GO TO LABEL.

The results are given in Table 9.3.

From the observed correlation between language level and block size, it follows that equations (9.1) and (9.2) are in agreement with generally held qualitative views.

VARIATION OF LEVEL BETWEEN LANGUAGES

In a general way, it is to be expected that the more powerful a general purpose language is, the greater the number of ways in which it can be

Table 9.3
Language Level λ vs Block Size β for a Set
of Fortran Programs

Program	η_1	η_2	N_2	N	ν	λ	β
(1)	10	21	50	108	0	3.78	108
(2)	13	6	29	71	1	0.31	36
(3)	23	54	228	510	11	1.36	42
(4)	20	13	37	104	7	0.65	13
(5)	17	14	51	121	4	0.63	24
(6)	15	13	41	101	2	0.87	34
(7)	12	6	21	73	4	0.69	15
(8)	16	17	60	141	4	0.89	28
(9)	25	46	150	324	8	1.20	36
(10)	10	9	24	55	2	1.31	18
(11)	10	9	29	66	2	1.08	22
(12)	11	9	32	72	2	0.81	24
(13)	12	9	32	73	2	0.70	24
(14)	11	20	81	170	2	1.70	57

coefficient of correlation between λ and β: 0.90

used for a given purpose. Since many of these different ways are also at different levels, it follows that as the mean value of λ increases, the variance about that mean will also increase. Since this statement constitutes a testable hypothesis, it suggests an additional experiment.

In addition to that hypothesis, however, a more fundamental one is also implied, to the effect that the mean or average value of λ, observed over a number of programs, does indeed show a quantitative increase with languages of increasing power. In order to test this second hypothesis, it is necessary to have an intuitively ordered list of languages. This requirement is immediately suspect, since it depends on whose intuition is involved. Almost certainly, however, the generally held view that assembly language is lower than Fortran, that Fortran is lower than PL/I, and that English itself is even higher must be accepted as the correct ordering. Consequently, both of these hypotheses may be tested with one experiment.

The values of η_1, η_2, N_2, and N for programs in five languages, and for 34 passages in English have been taken from two sources. The values for English were reported by Kulm, and those for PL/I, Algol 58, Fortran, Pilot (Purdue Instructional Language for Operating systems and Translators), and Compass (the assembly language of the Control Data 6500) were reported by Zweben. (Note: Pilot is a very low-level machine independent language.) The Zweben sample was chosen quite deliberately, because it consists of the same group of algorithms implemented in each of the five languages by one individual. Consequently, it should provide a homogeneous sample well-suited to the experiment to be performed.

With respect to the sample of English prose, this condition does not apply. Consequently, its ranking relative to the programming languages does not carry the same degree of confidence. Kulm's sample of English prose, however, covers a set of passages designed to represent a wide range in ease of comprehension; they were selected on this basis. It might be worth noting that the twelve technical abstracts discussed in Chapter 13 give a mean value of language level 7.4% higher than the mean of Kulm's passages, if redundancy is ignored.

While the individual test samples are small, ranging from 7 to 34 programs or passages per language, they demonstrate the expected effect, as can be seen in Table 9.4.

The percentage of programs of each language that have values of λ computed with equation (9.2) that fall within various class intervals is given in Table 9.5, and shown graphically in Figure 9.1.

Table 9.4
Mean and Variance of Language Level
for Seven Languages

Language	λ	Variance
English	2.16	0.74
PL/I	1.53	0.92
Algol 58	1.21	0.74
Fortran	1.14	0.81
Pilot	0.92	0.43
Assembly	0.88	0.42

From the experimental evidence, the simple language level relationship of equation (9.1) appears to be valid.

SIGNIFICANCE OF LANGUAGE LEVEL

For some two decades, an important part of the effort in the field of programming languages has been devoted to the design and implementation of new languages, and in each individual case that effort has been intended to provide an improvement over previously existing languages. However, because there has been no quantitative and economical method for measurement, deciding whether or not any improvement has in fact resulted has always been a highly subjective matter.

Table 9.5
Frequency Distributions of Language Levels for Different Languages

λ	Compass	Pilot	Fortran	Algol 58	PL/I	English
0.00 to 0.49	14%	14%	14%	14%	14%	0%
0.50 to 0.99	57	64	43	29	29	0
1.00 to 1.49	14	14	29	36	21	23
1.50 to 1.99	14	0	7	14	14	17
2.00 to 2.49	0	7	0	0	21	27
2.50 to 2.99	0	0	0	0	0	17
3.00 to 3.49	0	0	0	7	0	10
3.49 to 3.99	0	0	7	0	7	7

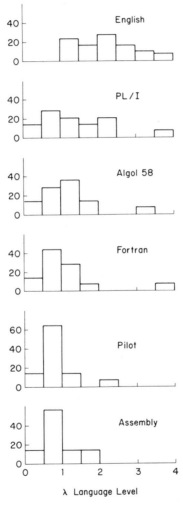

Figure 9.1 Frequency Distributions of λ

Without any hypothesis relating a particular language facility to the mental effort required to use it, there could be no absolute method for determining whether its contribution was positive or negative. A decade ago Garrett was able to show that a computer center is not warranted in adopting a new language unless it would provide more than a 38% improvement in programming productivity. However, at that time there was no way to estimate productivity as a function of language. By combining equation (9.1) with the effort equation of Chapter 7, it follows that the number of elementary mental discriminations required to write any program should follow an "inverse square law" with respect to language level, or

$$E = \frac{V^{*3}}{\lambda^2} \tag{9.14}$$

Therefore it should be possible to determine a mean λ from a small sample of test programs in each of two languages, and from them obtain relative productivities.

With respect to programming in any particular language, the last decade has witnessed a comparable effort devoted to improving programmer productivity by refinements in programming style. Here again, the lack of an effort-related measure of language level has made it, if not impossible, at least impossibly difficult to determine which particular components of any general style or technique were most worthwhile.

Additional significance that can be derived from the language level also follows from equation (9.14). As will be discussed in the next chapter, since both the potential volume, V^* and the mean value of λ must be known or calculable as soon as a programming project is specified and a language selected, a rational basis does exist for scheduling programming time.

Part II APPLICATIONS OF SOFTWARE THEORY

There are those who find any unexpected relationship in any branch of science to be intellectually fascinating in its own right, without regard for either potential utility or lack of it. Upon them we must rely for the future refinement, improvement, and deeper understanding so certainly needed in the area introduced in Part I of this monograph.

On the other hand, there are also those to whom the intellectual challenge lies not in the phenomena itself, but in its potential usefulness for the solution of difficult problems of a practical nature. Although a certain amount of overlap between theory and application is inevitable, the remainder of this monograph is devoted to this second point of view.

Quantitative equations for predicting the duration and error rates to be expected in programming tasks are among the most exciting results obtained by application of the theory, and these are dealt with in Chapters 10 and 11. In a more fundamental way, however, the application to English prose described in Chapter 13 may be of more lasting importance.

Chapter 10

Obtaining Length and
Programming Time
from Starting Conditions

A rather practical problem encountered in industrial or commercial computer work is the prediction of how many man-hours, or man-years, of programming time will be required to complete a proposed task. Although it is true that at least one fifty man-year project has been completed on schedule and on budget, schedule slippage is neither unknown nor even extremely rare in this area. In the commercial field some systematic methods of "sizing" proposed jobs have been developed, and they must not be discounted, despite the fact that they rely on *ad hoc* rules of thumb. But even when a job is brought on-line ahead of schedule, there is no dependable way to know whether it resulted from outstanding programming, or an over-generous schedule.

A similar but less serious problem is the accurate estimation of the ultimate size of a proposed program. At some point the program may exceed space available to it, requiring undesirable planning adjustments. Consequently, just as mechanical engineering applies the science of thermodynamics to the design of heat engines, the field of software engineering should be able to apply software science in solving these two specific problems.

Part I was concerned with several different relationships among various software parameters. In most cases, those relationships were applicable only after an algorithm had been implemented in some language, so that the basic software parameters, η_1, η_2, N_1 and N_2 could be counted. In that form, however, they do not yield equations that can be used to predict results of implementing a program at the time that actual programming is started.

Now, it appears to be true that any two independent properties are sufficient to determine all the others, in the absence of impurities, variations in fluency, in degree of concentration, or in Stroud number. Further, two of these independent properties should be known before the writing or programming actually starts. These two independent properties are the number of conceptually unique argument and result operands η_2^* and the language level to be employed λ. The first of these must be available as soon as a complete problem statement exists, and the mean and variance of λ should be available as soon as an implementation language has been selected.

Consequently, it is the aim of this chapter to express each parameter of interest in terms of η_2^* and λ. In most cases iteration is required, since solutions in closed form do not exist. Hence, the equations required for a computer solution will be derived first, and a graphical solution will be shown.

OBTAINING η_1 FROM η_2^* AND λ

Without any further assumptions, the equations derived in earlier chapters are adequate to determine the unique value of η_1 corresponding to any single values of η_2^* and λ prevailing simultaneously. The algebraic manipulation required is rather laborious, and basically dull. In this case, however, we will attempt to make it a bit more interesting by demonstrating that all that is required is the mechanical process of removing each of the six impurity classes of Chapter 7 from the following set of seven simultaneous equations.

In this case the equation number appearing on the left refers to the appearance of that equation in an earlier chapter. Since the seven equations contain a total of nine variables, the task is possible. The equations are

(9.1) $\lambda = LV^*$ (10.1)

(5.1) $L = V^*/V$ (10.2)

(3.1) $V = N \log_2 (\eta_1 + \eta_2)$ (10.3)

(3.4) $V^* = (2 + \eta_2^*) \log_2 (2 + \eta_2^*)$ (10.4)

(3.6) $V^{**} = (2 + \eta_2^* \log_2 \eta_2^*) \log_2 (2 + \eta_2^*)$ (10.5)

(4.7) $\eta_2 = (V^{**}/V^* - 1)(\eta_1 - 2) + \eta_2^*$ (10.6)

(2.7) $N = \eta_1 \log_2 \eta_1 + \eta_2 \log_2 \eta_2$ (10.7)

Impurities of two classes occur in the set as it stands, (common subexpressions, impurity IV, and unwarranted assignments, impurity V) and a third (unfactored expressions, impurity VI) will appear during the processing through the following eight steps.

STEP (1)

Note common subexpression (impurity IV) in (10.4) and (10.5), and generate

$$\text{TEMP} = 2 + \eta_2{}^*$$

or

$$\eta^* = 2 + \eta_2{}^* \tag{10.8}$$

STEP (2)

Eliminate common subexpression by replacing (10.4) and (10.5) with

$$V^* = \eta^* \log_2 \eta^* \tag{10.9}$$

and

$$V^{**} = (2 + \eta_2{}^* \log_2 \eta_2{}^*) \log_2 \eta^* \tag{10.10}$$

STEP (3)

Note unwarranted assignment (impurity V) in (10.2), and eliminate by replacing (10.1) and (10.2) with

$$(V^*)^2 = \lambda V \tag{10.11}$$

STEP (4)

Note unwarranted assignment in (10.3), and eliminate by replacing (10.3) and (10.11) by

$$(V^*)^2 = \lambda N \log_2 (\eta_1 + \eta_2) \tag{10.12}$$

STEP (5)

Note unwarranted assignment in (10.7) and eliminate by replacing (10.7) and (10.12) by

$$(V^*)^2 = \lambda (\eta_1 \log_2 \eta_1 + \eta_2 \log_2 \eta_2) \log_2 (\eta_1 + \eta_2) \tag{10.13}$$

STEP (6)

Note unwarranted assignment in (10.10) and eliminate by replacing (10.6) and (10.10) by

$$\eta_2 = \left(\frac{(2 + \eta_2{}^* \log_2 \eta_2{}^*) \log_2 \eta^*)}{V^*} -1 \right)(\eta_1 - 2) + \eta_2{}^* \tag{10.14}$$

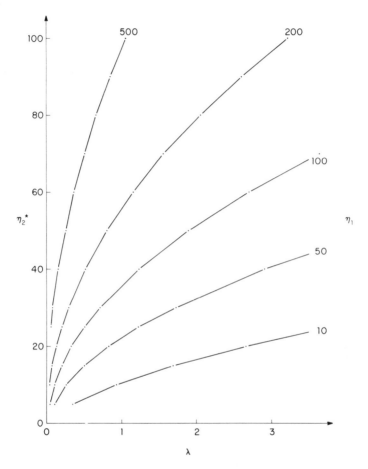

Figure 10.1   Unique Operators

At this point the four remaining equations, (10.8), (10.9), (10.13), and (10.14), do not contain any instances of impurities (I) through (V), but the calculation of $L \times V$ for the four equations yields 17, whereas the theoretical value based on an η_2^* of 3(λ, η_2^*, η_1) is 12. This discrepancy indicates the possible presence of an unfactored expression, impurity VI.

STEP (7)

Detect and remove the unfactored expression (impurity VI) by replacing (10.14) with

$$\eta_2 = \eta_2{}^* \log_2 (\eta^*/2) (\eta_1 - 2)/\eta^* + \eta_2{}^* \qquad (10.15)$$

STEP (8)

Note unwarranted assignment in (10.9) and eliminate by replacing (10.9) and (10.13) by

$$(\eta^* \log_2 \eta^*)^2 =$$
$$\lambda(\eta_1 \log_2 \eta_1 + \eta_2 \log_2 \eta_2) \log_2 (\eta_1 + \eta_2) \qquad (10.16)$$

At this point the original seven equations have been reduced to three, (10.8), (10.15), and (10.16), and both $\hat{N}$ and $L \times V$ are within about

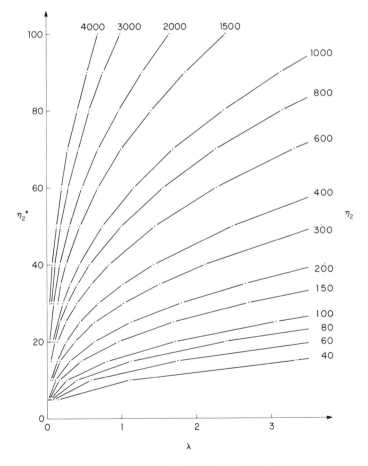

Figure 10.2   Unique Operands

10% of their theoretical values. It is of interest to note that six of the original eleven operands have been removed, and that one new one has been added.

Using equations (10.8), (10.15), and (10.16), then, it is possible to obtain a plot of η_1 as a function of $\eta_2{}^*$ and λ, as shown in figure 10.1.

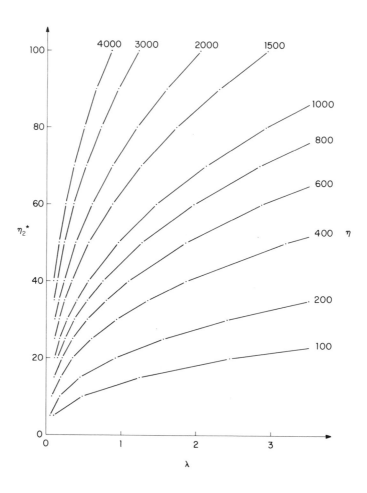

Figure 10.3   Vocabulary

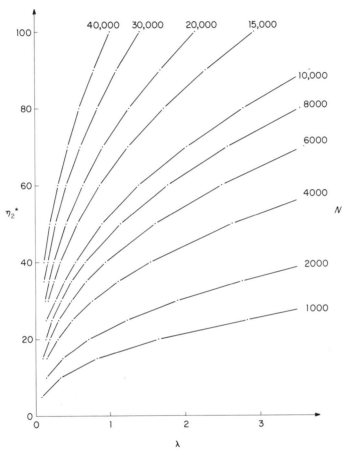

Figure 10.4   Program Length

OBTAINING PROGRAM VOCABULARY AND LENGTH
FROM η_2^* AND λ

Once the value of η_1 corresponding to any pair of values of η_2^* and λ is determined, η_2 may be obtained directly from equation (10.15), with the results as shown in figure 10.2. Figure 10.3 shows the plot of the functional relationship for the sum of η_1 and η_2, or the vocabulary η.

Similarly, with η_1 and η_2 determined, the program length N may be determined directly from equation (10.7), as shown in figure 10.4.

Using figure 10.4, it is possible to obtain estimates of the lengths that unwritten programs would require in different languages, on the basis of nothing more than a complete, nonprocedural problem statement. While it is a basic premise of the preceding chapters that program length is fundamentally measured in units of N, rather than in number of statements, sentences, or instructions; it is still true that for any specific

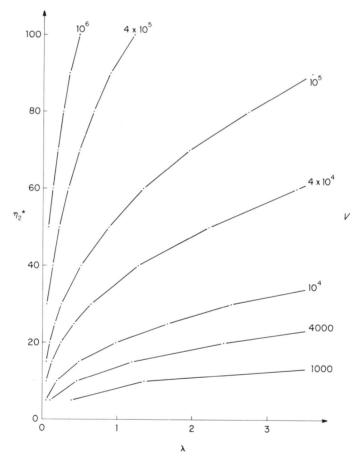

Figure 10.5   Program Volume—Bits

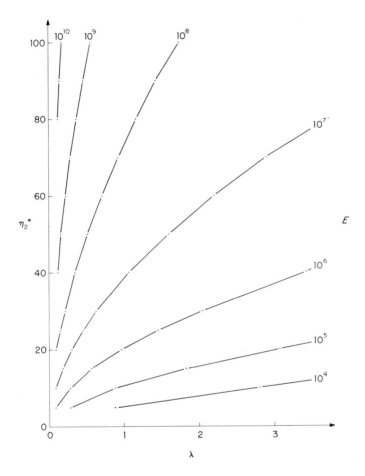

Figure 10.6   Programming Effort—Discriminations

language the correlation between N and such an earlier unit is quite high. Consequently, it is possible to convert from the generality of figure 10.4 to, say, number of statements for a particular language.

Another potential use for figure 10.4 is the following. For a program to be written at a given level in a machine independent language, and then compiled into a given machine language, it is possible to obtain estimates of the length both before and after compilation. The latter requires only a knowledge of the average language level λ of programs produced by a given compiler. From the limited study available to date, it appears that compiler generated code is of a slightly lower language level than hand-written assembly language. Indeed, it has been suggested, but not yet confirmed, that this difference may provide a useful measure of the figure of merit of a given compiler, and that for a particular computer, the language level of hand-coded assembly language may be useful in differentiating between alternative repertoires of instructions.

In any event, for most computers it is a simple task to convert from program length in units of N to units of number of instructions, bytes, or words. It should be noted, however, that the program length obtained in this way is independent of the sizes of data areas. While the number of unique items in a data area will be η_2, as obtained from figure 10.2, the lengths of arrays or tables are not known functions of any of the basic parameters.

OBTAINING PROGRAMMING EFFORT AND TIME FROM η_2^* AND λ

The number of elementary mental discriminations E required to implement a given algorithm can also be expressed in terms of η_2^* and λ directly. In the effort equation (8.2), or

$$E = V/L \tag{10.17}$$

we may substitute for L from equation (10.2), obtaining

$$E = V^2/V^* \tag{10.18}$$

Then substituting for V from equation (10.11) yields

$$E = (V^*)^3/\lambda^2 \tag{10.19}$$

which may be expanded with equation (10.4).

This variation of effort with η_2^* and λ is shown graphically in figure 10.6. Here again, in addition to its obvious employment in terms of language comparison and job sizing, this figure can be used to obtain quantitative estimates of the contribution of a given compiler to the human effort of programming. The relationships derived and tested in Chapter 8 can now be extended to permit prediction of programming times from η_2^* and λ, rather than from parameters only available after a program has been written. Under the conditions that (1) a complete but nonprocedural problem statement is available, (2) high concentration

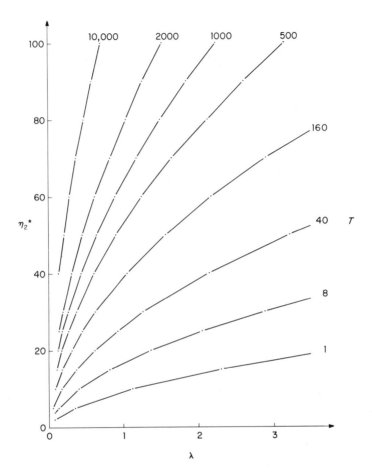

Figure 10.7 Programming Time—Hours

exists, and (3) fluency in the selected language exists, then equation (8.4), or

$$T = E/S \qquad\qquad (10.20)$$

requires only a value of the Stroud number S to obtain units of time from the number of elementary discriminations, E, of equation (10.20) and figure 10.6. Figure 10.7 shows this relationship of programming time to $\eta_2{}^*$ and λ for a Stroud number of 18 discriminations per second.

Chapter 11

The Error Hypothesis

A highly significant fraction of the time and effort required to implement most computer programs is devoted to "debugging" them, or detecting and eliminating errors of commission or omission introduced during the initial writing phase. Consequently, any insight that can be obtained regarding the initial number of errors to be expected in a given program will offer promise of practical importance.

In this chapter, we show that software relationships do provide a method for estimating the number of initial errors to be expected in a given program. The method is quantitative and subject to statistical variation. Since it predicts only the initial number of errors, it does not converge as these errors are removed. Therefore, it does not offer a "proof of correctness" in the mathematical sense, but gives a confidence level in the engineering sense.

It was shown in Chapter 8 that the amount of time required to implement a computer program depends on the number of elementary mental discriminations E that it requires. As a consequence, it follows that the number of points at which it is possible to make an erroneous discrimination is also given by the value of E. A demonstration that programming error rates are highly correlated with values of E would therefore constitute another confirmation of the predictive capability of the theory. While such a demonstration is given later in this chapter, it would be even more impressive, and satisfying, if the quantitative relationship between discriminations and errors could be derived and tested. This will be done in the following sections.

DERIVATION OF THE ERROR EQUATION

In order to deal with error rates in programming, it is necessary to have a definition of such errors. While the number of possible definitions may have a finite upper bound, it must nevertheless be quite large. For present purposes, however, any objective definition for which data are available may suffice. Accordingly, we will accept the intuitively satisfying definition of Bell and Sullivan, and restrict the following discussion to "delivered bugs'', where the term ''delivered'' refers to bugs remaining in a program implementation after completion of some identifiable phase, such as publication. It should be noted that the term ''delivered'' does not imply that this phase coincides with delivery to an ultimate customer. Rather, it will be interpreted as applying to an earlier stage, such as delivery of a module of a system for integration with other modules. Letting this *total number of delivered bugs* in a given implementation be represented by the symbol B, the problem reduces to the derivation of an expression for B in terms of the basic software parameters.

Let us start by assuming that the psychologists are correct in suggesting that the human brain can handle (i.e., produce a result from) five ''chunks'' in its high speed memory. Let E_{crit} represent this capability, and obtain its software value in the following way.

Let each ''chunk'', as well as the result, contribute one to the number of conceptually unique operands in a potential language. That is to say, $\eta_2{}^* = 6$. Since $\eta_1{}^* = 2$, this gives, since

$$V^* = (\eta_1{}^* + \eta_2{}^*)\log_2(\eta_1{}^* + \eta_2{}^*) \tag{11.1}$$

the value

$$V^*_{crit} = (2 + 6)\log_2(2\,2 + 6) = 24 \tag{11.2}$$

Now from equation (10.19) we have

$$E = (V^*)^3/\lambda^2 \tag{11.3}$$

and from Table 9.4 we have for English the value $\lambda = 2.16$. The assumption of five ''chunks'', combined with the language level of English then yields

$$E_{crit} = (24)^3/(2.16)^2 = 3000 \tag{11.4}$$

which may be tested in a number of ways. In order to separate the distinct aspects of the derivation, however, we will hold the result above for later use.

Now let us define E_0 as the *mean number of elementary discriminations between potential errors in programming,* and B as the number of delivered errors in a program. At first it might appear that we should expect

$$B = E/E_0 \tag{11.5}$$

but this would not allow for any similarity or redundancy in the material being generated.

Conveniently, the program level L is in a proper sense a measure of this redundancy. Note that it is only in a potential language, in which any program can be expressed as a procedure call, that there will be absolutely no repetition of either operators or operands. For such a potential language, L is equal to one. For all others, L will decrease in proportion to the increase in redundancy.

Consequently, instead of equation (11.5), we should expect that

$$B = L\frac{E}{E_0} \tag{11.6}$$

But since, from equation (8.2)

$$E = V/L \tag{11.7}$$

it follows algebraically that the product LE may be replaced by V, giving

$$B = V/E_0 \tag{11.8}$$

Frequently, however, values of E rather than V are more readily available. Noting from equation (10.11) that

$$V = (V^*)^2/\lambda \tag{11.9}$$

and from equation (10.19) that

$$E = (V^*)^3/\lambda^2 \tag{11.10}$$

we may solve both (11.9) and (11.10) for V^*, equate, and obtain

$$(\lambda V)^{1/2} = (\lambda^2 E)^{1/3} \tag{11.11}$$

or

$$V = \lambda^{1/3} E^{2/3} \tag{11.12}$$

Now since the cube root of any number close to one is even closer to one, for most programming languages the λ term may be ignored, giving

$$B = E^{2/3}/E_0 \tag{11.13}$$

where equation (11.13) should give a close approximation to equation (11.8). (At this point, it is interesting to note the similarity in both function and value of the exponent 2/3 and the exponents in typical "learning curve equations" used to predict the effect of "economy of scale" in industry.)

If we now equate the term E_0 in equations (11.8) and (11.13) with the value of E_{crit} found in equation (11.4), we have the testable relations

$$\hat{B} = E^{2/3}/3000 \tag{11.14}$$

and

$$\hat{B} = V/3000 \tag{11.15}$$

where the hat has been placed over the number of bugs to differentiate between estimates (or predictions) and observed counts.

VALIDATION OF THE ERROR EQUATION
WITH BELL AND SULLIVAN'S DATA

Bell and Sullivan have reported on a most ingenious study that they conducted on errors in computer programs. While their complete study was most comprehensive, that part of it which concerns us here can be explained quite simply. They selected as test data those algorithms that had been both published and subsequently certified in the series printed in the Communications of the Association for Computing Machinery. They then classified these programs into two groups, depending on whether the certification found zero errors, or reported a definite error correction required. They ignored those cases in which an error could be attributed to typography. They then sampled programs from both the error-free and the erroneous classes, and among other tests, they obtained values of the software length N. With respect to the latter, which they denoted by H, they wrote

> First, Halstead length alone appears to be an excellent predictor of correctness. No correct program had H greater than 237, and only one erroneous program, algorithm R, had H less than 284. It would seem that the editor of the Algorithms section would do well not to accept, or at least to require special prepublication certification, of any algorithm whose Halstead length exceeds, say, 260.

In order to test the relationship of equation (11.15) against the value of $N = 260$ quoted above, we may proceed as follows. First, the volume of a program that is just as likely to have zero errors as it is to have one or more may be obtained by setting B equal to one-half in equation (11.15), and solving for V. This gives

$$V = BE_{\text{crit}} = 0.5 \times 3000 = 1500 \tag{11.16}$$

In order to obtain the length from the volume, we note from equation (3.1) that

$$V = N \log_2 \eta \qquad (11.17)$$

and from equation (2.7) that

$$N = \eta_1 \log_2 \eta_1 + \eta_2 \log_2 \eta_2 \qquad (11.18)$$

From equation (11.18) it follows that for η_1 equal to η_2

$$N = \eta \log_2 (\eta/2) \qquad (11.19)$$

and in case η_1 is not equal to η_2, equation (11.19) is still a close approximation to equation (11.18). For example, if $\eta_2 = 3 \times \eta_1$, the error in equation (11.19) will be less than 4% in the range involved. Consequently, we may substitute equation (11.19) for N in equation (11.17) giving

$$V = \eta \log_2 (\eta/2) \log_2 \eta \qquad (11.20)$$

For $V = 1500$, as obtained in equation (11.16), equation (11.20) requires a value of $\eta = 54.52$. Supplying this value in equation (11.19) gives

$$N = 54.52 \log_2 (54.52/2) = 259.99 \qquad (11.21)$$

where the accidental closeness in agreement between the derived value and the much less precise value reported by Bell and Sullivan should not be allowed to becloud the basic, though imprecise, agreement between the hypothesis and the experiment. In fact, we note that if instead of using the psychologists' value of 5 "chunks" to derive the length of error-free programs, we had used Bell and Sullivan's value to obtain the number of "chunks", a value of 5.02 would have resulted, with a value of 1499.9 for V_{crit}.

VALIDATION OF THE ERROR EQUATION
WITH AKIYAMA'S DATA

At the International Federation of Information Processing Societies Congress in 1971, F. Akiyama published a superb set of data on the nine modules of a large system implemented in Japan. Akiyama reported that complete implementation of the system required approximately 100 man-months, and presented the data reproduced in Table 11.1.

While the data of Table 11.1 do not include the four basic software parameters directly, they do supply observations from which it is possible to estimate them quite closely.

Table 11.1
Akiyama's Published Data

Program module	Program steps (S)	Decisions (D)	SR calls (J)	Number of bugs (B)
MA	4032	372	283	102
MB	1329	215	49	18
MC	5453	552	362	146
MD	1674	111	130	26
ME	2051	315	197	71
MF	2513	217	186	37
MG	699	104	32	16
MH	3792	233	110	50
MX	3412	416	230	80

Merely assuming that each of the S machine language steps includes one operator and one operand gives

$$N_2 = S \tag{11.22}$$

and

$$N = 2S \tag{11.23}$$

Now the number of unique operators η_1 for machine language programs is composed of three distinct components. The first of these are the operators selected from the machine's repertoire of instructions. For large programs, this component may be roughly approximated as an octal hundred, or 64. Second is the number of distinct operations provided by functions or subroutines. This component should correspond to item J in Table 11.1. Finally, each transfer to a unique location contributes directly tp η_1. Since the number of transfers implied by item D in Table 11.1 do not each involve transfer to a *unique* location, only a fraction, perhaps one third, should contribute to η_1. We then have, roughly

$$\eta_1 = (D/3) + J + 64 \tag{11.24}$$

At this point, we need only a value of η_2 to be able to calculate E. Since we have both η_1 and N, the length relation or equation (11.18), will yield solutions for the missing η_2. With these relationships, Akiyama's

Table 11.2
Software Parameters Calculated from Observations in Table 11.1

Module	MA	MB	MC	MD	ME	MF	MG	MH	MX
N	8064	2658	10906	3348	4102	5026	1398	7584	6824
N_2	4032	1329	5453	1674	2051	2513	699	3792	3412
η_1	471	180	610	231	366	322	131	252	433
η_2	442	176	574	201	138	287	76	603	357

observations from Table 11.1 give the basic software parameters shown in Table 11.2.

The effort E and number of bugs $\hat{B}$ have been calculated from the values in Table 11.2 using the equations

$$E = V/L = \frac{N \log_2 (\eta_1 + \eta_2)}{2\eta_2/\eta_1 N_2} \qquad (11.25)$$

and

$$\hat{B} = E^{2/3}/3000 \qquad (11.14)$$

Table 11.3
Observed and Predicted Errors
for Akiyama's Data

Program Module	E (millions)	$\hat{B}$	B (observed)
MG	6	12	16
MB	15	21	18
MD	28	31	26
MF	66	54	37
MH	59	50	50
ME	100	72	71
MX	136	88	80
MA	170	102	102
MC	323	157	146
SUM	903	587	546

The results, arranged in order of increasing errors, are given in Table 11.3.

It is apparent that equation (11.14) represents Akiyama's data with considerable fidelity. Further, as mentioned at the beginning of this chapter, the correlation between observed errors and the total number of opportunities for error E is nearly as high. As an added check on the consistency of the values in Table 11.3, one might compare the predicted programming time with that observed. As observation, we have Akiyama's mention of "Man-hours needed for production and inspection were about 100 man-months."

For the theory, we need only to divide the sum of the discriminations E by the Stroud number. If we take a man-month as consisting of four and one-sixth man-weeks of 40 hours each, then it contains 600,000 seconds. At 18 discriminations per second, this gives 10.8 million discriminations per man-month for S. Therefore, E/S is 903/10.8 or 84 man-months, which is in reasonable agreement with the observation.

The apparent agreement of the hypothesis with both the Bell and Sullivan data and the Akiyama data suggests that even in an area as esoteric as programming error rates, the simple theoretical framework may provide useful insight. On the other hand, it should be clear that such insight as it may provide will be useful only to the extent that it is used in further study of this complex area.

Chapter 12

Modularity

The problem of optimum modularization is not yet well understood, but it may be attacked from at least four different directions. These four approaches may be characterized as

(1) Equalization of length.
(2) Minimization of modular potential volume.
(3) Limiting length of error-free programs.
(4) The psychological concept of "chunks."

In the following sections, each of these approaches will be investigated. While each investigation approaches the optimum modularization problem from a totally different point of view, it will be found that on completion they yield surprisingly consistent quantitative results.

Defining M as the *number of modules* in a program, it is reasonable to expect that for any particular program there should be an optimum value of M, and that for programs of sufficient length that value should be greater than one. The problem, then, is to find a relation between M and other properties of an implementation.

An interesting possibility stems from the finding of Chapter 2 that the length relationship holds for logically distinct modules as well as for complete programs, despite its nonlinear nature. This possibility is explored in the next section.

EQUALIZATION OF LENGTH

If, as in equation (11.19), we express the length equation for a complete program in terms of its total vocabulary rather than unique operators and operands, then we have

$$N = \eta \log_2 (\eta/2) \qquad (12.1)$$

Now if we let η_m represent the vocabulary of each of M modules, and N_m represent its length, we have

92

$$N_m = \eta_m \log_2 (\eta_m/2) \tag{12.2}$$

and we need a relation between η_m, M, and η. Since η_m must be smaller than η for any M greater than one, and because there must be a certain amount of duplication or overlap, it follows that

$$\frac{\eta}{M} \leq \eta_m \leq \eta \tag{12.3}$$

More specifically, if the η elements are divided into two classes, say a and b, in such a way that η_a represents those which must be present in all modules, then

$$\eta_m = \eta_a + (\eta - \eta_a)/M \tag{12.4}$$

where it is only necessary to obtain a relation for η_a. In considering the question of which, or more simply, how many of the η vocabulary elements must be present in each and every module, we would expect this to be related to the potential volume of the algorithm. Accordingly, if we assume that η_a may be represented by η^*, equation (12.4) becomes

$$\eta_m = \eta^* + (\eta - \eta^*)/M \tag{12.5}$$

and equation (12.2) becomes

$$N_m = \left(\eta^* + \frac{\eta - \eta^*}{M} \right) \log_2 \left(\frac{\eta^* + (\eta - \eta^*)/M}{2} \right) \tag{12.6}$$

Now since

$$N = MN_m \tag{12.7}$$

we have the relationship

$$\eta \log_2 (\eta/2) = M \left(\frac{(\eta - \eta^*)}{M} + \eta^* \right) \log_2 \left(\frac{(\eta - \eta^*)/M}{2} \right) \tag{12.8}$$

which contains only the three variables, η, η^*, and M. Since for any specified language, or value of λ, η^* determines η, it must also determine M.

Studying equation (12.8), we find that for any value of η^* and a corresponding value of η, there will be two values of M that satisfy it. The first of these is, of course, $M = 1$. The second, on the other hand, is the value of interest, and it will increase as η^* increases. Letting $\lambda = 1$,

Table 12.1
Number of Modules Obtained by Equating Length
to Sum of Modular Lengths

$\eta_2{}^*$	η	M	$\eta_2{}^*$	η	M	$\eta_2{}^*$	η	M
2	8.76	0.49	18	157	2.89	34	476	5.71
4	18.16	0.78	20	188	3.23	36	527	6.07
6	29.93	1.04	22	221	3.58	38	582	6.44
8	44.42	1.32	24	257	3.92	40	638	6.81
10	61.59	1.61	26	296	4.27	42	697	7.18
12	81.53	1.92	28	337	4.63	44	759	7.55
14	104.14	2.24	30	381	4.99	46	824	7.92
16	129.47	2.56	32	427	5.35	48	891	8.30

and obtaining η^*, η pairs as in Chapter 10, the values of M satisfying equation (12.8) are shown in Table 12.1.

The results of Table 12.1 will be compared with other approaches after the latter have been investigated.

MINIMIZATION OF MODULAR POTENTIAL VOLUME

In considering modularization, it is apparent that the smallest module that might be useful would have two inputs and one output, for an $\eta_2{}^*$ of 3. But if all programs were partioned into modules of such small size, the overhead involved would be too great.

Letting $V_M{}^*$ represent the *combined potential volume* of a modularized program, and $V_m{}^*$ represent the *individual potential volume* of the average module, then we might expect

$$V_M{}^* = MV_m{}^* + M \log_2 M \qquad (12.9)$$

where the last term on the right represents that overhead. Expressing the individual potential volume as

$$V_m{}^* = (\eta_1{}^* + \eta_2{}^*/M) \log_2 (\eta_1{}^* + \eta_2{}^*/M) \qquad (12.10)$$

and setting $\eta_1{}^*$ equal to 2 allows equation (12.9) to be expressed as

$$V_M{}^* = M((2 + \eta_2{}^*/M) \log_2 (2 + \eta_2{}^*/M) + \log_2 M) \qquad (12.11)$$

Now for any given value of $\eta_2{}^*$, there will be a value for number of

Table 12.2
Number of Modules M Providing
Minimum Potential Volume
from Equation (12.11)

$\eta_2{}^*$	M	$\eta_2{}^*$	M	$\eta_2{}^*$	M
2	0.5	18	2.9	34	4.9
4	0.9	20	3.1	36	5.1
6	1.2	22	3.4	38	5.4
8	1.5	24	3.6	40	5.6
10	1.8	26	3.9	42	5.8
12	2.1	28	4.1	44	6.1
14	2.3	30	4.4	46	6.3
16	2.6	32	4.6	48	6.5

modules M for which equation (12.11) gives a minimum for the combined modular potential volume $V_M{}^*$. For a range of values of $\eta_2{}^*$, values of M yielding these minima are shown in Table 12.2.

Again, consideration of the results in Table 12.2 are postponed until they can be compared with others.

MODULES AS ERROR-FREE PROGRAMS

In addition to their determination that $N = 260$ represented an upper boundary for error-free programs published in the Communications of the Association for Computing Machinery, Bell and Sullivan also calculated the average length of correct programs in that series.

If we adopt the simple assumption that the ideal module size should have a length equal to the mean length of error-free programs, then Bell and Sullivan's observations may be used to obtain it. They reported that $\overline{N} = 161.9$, for a sample predominantly in Algol. Using $\lambda = 1.21$ from Table 9.4 for Algol 58, and the equations of Chapter 10, this gives a value of $\eta_2{}^*$ of 7.76.

Using this approach, we should expect that

$$M = \eta_2{}^*/7.76 \qquad (12.12)$$

which will be compared with the other approaches shortly.

Table 12.3
Number of Modules as a Function of η_2* Using Four Different Methods

η_2*	(1) Length Equalization [Eq. (12.8)] $M(1)$	(2) Potential Volume [Eq. (12.11)] $M(2)$	(3) Error-Free Programs [Eq. (12.12)] $M(3)$	(4) Psychology "Chunks" [Eq. (12.13)] $M(4)$
2	0.5	0.5	0.3	0.3
4	0.8	0.9	0.5	0.7
6	1.0	1.2	0.8	1.0
8	1.3	1.5	1.0	1.3
10	1.6	1.8	1.3	1.7
12	1.9	2.1	1.5	2.0
14	2.2	2.3	1.8	2.3
16	2.6	2.6	2.1	2.7
18	2.9	2.9	2.3	3.0
20	3.2	3.1	2.6	3.3
22	3.6	3.4	2.8	3.7
24	3.9	3.6	3.1	4.0
26	4.3	3.9	3.4	4.3
28	4.6	4.1	3.6	4.7
30	5.0	4.4	3.9	5.0
32	5.4	4.4	4.1	5.3
34	5.7	4.9	4.4	5.7
36	6.1	5.1	4.6	6.0
38	6.4	5.4	4.9	6.3
40	6.8	5.6	5.2	6.7
42	7.2	5.8	5.4	7.0
44	7.6	6.1	5.7	7.3
46	7.9	6.3	5.9	7.7
48	8.3	6.5	6.2	8.0

MODULE SIZE FROM "CHUNKS"

While the concept is not universally accepted in psychology, the hypothesis that the human brain organizes material in "chunks", and that the "high-speed portion" of the brain manipulates these "chunks" is well-known in that field. Further, those who place confidence in the hypothesis also postulate that five "chunks" can be manipulated simultaneously. If we tentatively accept this hypothesis (or perhaps more significantly, provide a methodology for testing it), then we have an additional approach to the quantitative definition of an optimum module size.

By definition, η_2^* is the number of conceptually unique input and output parameters involved in an algorithm, and it is a language-independent property. In this terminology, each of the five "chunks" must represent a conceptually unique input, and any result of such manipulation must correspond to a conceptually unique output parameter.

Consequently, for an ideal module, $\eta_2^* = 5 + 1 = 6$, and the number of modules in a program should be given by

$$M = \eta_2^*/6 \qquad (12.13)$$

As can be seen from Table 12.3, the four approaches considered, although each is dependent on a completely different starting point, arrive at virtually the same conclusion.

In fact, the almost precise agreement between methods (1) and (4) appear to suggest the existence of a deeper relationship than is apparent in the equations. Certainly it is difficult to imagine any correspondence between the concept that the length relationship should hold for the parts as well as for the whole, on the one hand, and the concept of "chunking" on the other hand. Over the range examined, however, both can be closely approximated by the single, simple relationship

$$M = \eta_2^*/6 \qquad (12.13)$$

and it appears that programs modularized accordingly will be the easiest to write, debug, comprehend, and maintain.

Chapter 13

Quantitative Analysis
of English Prose

The software relationships found for computer programs, as discussed in Chapters 1 through 12, appear to be reasonably independent of any particular computer language. This immediately suggests that the same relationships might also play a role in the structure of messages expressed in natural languages, such as English or Russian. Since the grammars of natural languages appear to be far more complicated than their computer counterparts, it would be only reasonable to suspect that such an analysis might introduce problems not previously encountered.

On the other hand, if the results for computer languages can be shown to extend to natural prose, then the power of the software theory will receive support in a much more general context. In this chapter, we present an outline of the first results obtained in this interesting area. The treatment depends primarily on methods devised by a mathematical linguist, Kulm, and independently tested by a psychologist, Kennedy. The data and analysis used here, however, have not previously appeared in the literature, and consequently every effort is made to include all pertinent details.

The first step, of course, is to define for prose an equivalent method of counting the basic software parameters.

IDENTIFICATION OF OPERATORS AND OPERANDS IN ENGLISH PROSE

For the machine language of a simple computer, the division of each instruction into an operator function code and an operand address provided a basic simplicity. The identification of operators and operands was relatively straightforward and unambiguous. At first sight, it would appear that no such simplicity applies to prose. If, for example, we count nouns as operands and verbs as operators, then the roles of other parts of speech are still undetermined.

It was Kulm who pointed out that this part of the problem had been solved long ago by Miller, Newman, and Friedman of Harvard. In 1958, they noted that all words in written English could be, and should be, divided into two classes. The first they called "function words", and the second, "content words". Quoting from their definitions:

> We will call these two classes the "function words" and the "content words". Function words include those which are traditionally called articles, prepositions, pronouns, conjunctions, and auxiliary verbs, plus certain irregular forms. The function words have rather specific syntactic functions which must, by and large, be known individually to the speaker of English. The content words include those which are traditionally called nouns, verbs, and adjectives, plus most of the adverbs. It is relatively easy to add new content words to a language, but the set of function words is much more resistant to innovations.

Miller and his colleagues then drew up a list of 363 function words in English, and demonstrated that classification based on a word's presence or absence in this list provided samples with distinctly different statistical properties. Their list, arranged by word length as in their original paper, is reproduced as Table 13.1.

In addition to the function words, the experience with computer languages suggests that punctuation symbols also serve as operators. By including capitalization as an operator, we have the program-consistent condition that no properly written sentence can contain fewer than two distinct operators, capitalization and period.

In the experiments that follow, then, all words that are not included in Table 13.1 are counted as operands. With respect to the occurrences of numbers, Miller noted a possible ambiguity. We resolve this ambiguity rather arbitrarily by classifying all numbers which contain more than one significant digit as operands, and the others as operators. For example, the numbers 1, 10, 200, and 5,000 are counted as operators, while 1.0, 12, and 1.2 are counted as operands.

While it may eventually be possible to improve on the list of Table 13.1 on the basis of further research, at this point it is more satisfying to retain the complete objectivity inherent in totally independent work completed two decades ago.

ESTIMATION OF AMOUNT OF REDUNDANCY

In prose of almost any sort a large amount of redundancy is usually present. While it may occur in various ways, the most obvious is in the use of a synonym to represent a given word that otherwise requires

Table 13.1
English Operators: The Function Words of Miller, Newman and Friedman

a	how	just	wilt	there	itself	insofar	thousand
I	its	keep	with	these	middle	instead	together
am	may	kept	your	thine	mighty	million	whatever
an	nay	less	about	thing	myself	neither	whenever
as	nor	lest	above	third	nobody	nothing	wherefor
at	not	many	after	those	others	nowhere	wherever
be	now	mine	again	three	please	outside	yourself
by	one	more	alive	truly	pretty	outward	aforesaid
do	our	most	alone	twice	rather	perhaps	elsewhere
he	own	much	along	under	really	seventy	forasmuch
if	per	must	alway	until	second	several	foregoing
in	she	next	among	wasnt	selves	sixteen	halfdozen
is	six	nine	apart	where	should	someday	otherwise
it	ten	noes	aside	which	theirs	thereby	ourselves
me	the	none	awful	while	thence	therein	something
my	thy	once	being	whose	things	thereof	sometimes
no	too	ones	below	would	thirds	thereon	shouldest
of	two	only	canst	yeses	thirty	thither	therefore
oh	was	onto	could	yours	though	through	therewith
on	way	ours	doing	across	thrice	thyself	twothirds
or	who	over	eight	almost	toward	undoing	wherefore
so	why	past	every	always	twelve	whereas	wherewith
to	yea	plus	fifty	amount	twenty	wherein	beforehand
up	yes	real	first	anyone	unless	whereof	everything
us	yet	same	forth	around	upward	whereon	everywhere
we	you	self	forty	awhile	weight	whether	fourteenth
ye	also	some	hence	before	whence	whither	henceforth
ado	anon	such	inner	behind	whilst	without	heretofore
all	away	than	later	beyond	withal	although	oftentimes
and	been	that	least	cannot	within	anything	themselves
any	both	thee	might	during	against	anywhere	thereafter
are	does	them	never	eighth	already	backward	throughout
but	done	then	ninth	eighty	another	eighteen	underneath
can	dont	they	often	either	anybody	evermore	yourselves
did	down	this	other	eleven	awfully	everyone	furthermore
etc	each	thou	ought	enough	because	fourteen	midthirties
few	else	thus	quite	except	between	inasmuch	theretofore
for	even	unto	right	fairly	farther	insomuch	twentyseven
get	ever	upon	seven	fourth	forever	likewise	backwardness
got	five	very	shall	hardly	forward	millenia	nevertheless
had	four	well	shalt	having	further	millions	whereinsoever
has	from	were	since	height	herself	moreover	
her	gets	what	sixth	herein	himself	nowadays	
hes	have	when	sixty	hither	howbeit	overmuch	
him	here	whom	still	indeed	however	somebody	
his	into	will	their	inward	hundred	somewhat	

repetition. This practice serves an obviously useful purpose in human communication. Consequently, in a practical sense, the frequent use of synonyms cannot be thought of as impure, despite the fact that in a technical sesne it is identical to the impurity III (synonymous operands, discussed in Chapter 7).

However, because the relationships discussed in previous chapters are based upon implementations of algorithms in nonredundant styles, it is necessary to allow for this practice in English or other natural languages.

This problem could be solved in either of two ways. The more direct consists of the complete analysis of any text under study, in order that all sets of synonyms could be counted as multiple occurrences of the same word. This method appears sound, but it has two important disadvantages. First, it is a most laborious process, not readily reduced to computerization. Second, it appears to be highly subjective. This results from the fact that two words that may be synonymous in one context may have distinct meanings in another. A further difficulty encountered in the application of the direct method arises when a given word is used with variations in number or tense.

An alternative solution to the redundancy problem, and the one that is used here, avoids the disadvantages discussed above. It is based on the mechanical tabulation of every distinct letter pattern in the text being analyzed, whether or not it is conceptually unique.

This produces a *gross vocabulary,* denoted by η', which must be reduced by the *fraction of redundancy k* to obtain the net, or standard vocabulary η so that

$$\eta = k\eta' \qquad (13.1)$$

A rough estimate of the average value of k is obtained in the following way. For every occurrence of a conceptually unique word, there is some probability that it will be used in both singular and plural forms. Second, there is some average probability that it will be accompanied by either a synonym or an antonym, and thirdly, there is the probability that it will appear in more than one tense. If each of these three probabilities is assigned the value one-half, then

$$\eta' = (1 + \frac{1}{2} + \frac{1}{2} + \frac{1}{2})\eta \qquad (13.2)$$

or

$$\hat{k} = \frac{1}{2.5} = 0.4 \qquad (13.3)$$

In the following experiments, this value of $k = 0.4$ will be used, but it should be noted that without further investigation, it must be considered as only an estimate. Furthermore, if the counting method were to be changed, then the value of k would also be changed. For example, if the word count does not distinguish between singular and plural, or if it ignores differences due to tense, then k should be higher. If the counting method became complete, grouping synonyms and antonyms as well, then we would have $k = 1$ and $\eta = \eta'$.

SELECTION OF TECHNICAL PROSE

As work on programming impurities later showed, the selection of an objectively chosen set of well-written algorithms for the initial validation of the length relation was of some help in avoiding the premature introduction of possible sources of variance. Consequently, it appears to be equally desirable to investigate initially the corresponding relationships for written English with a similar set of objectively selected passages.

Properties which such a set of passages should have may be obtained from several considerations. First, the works should consist of technical prose, in order that phenomena such as poetic allegory and meter not cloud the experiment. Second, it appears desirable that each passage in the set be complete in itself, in order to avoid possible effects of modularity. Third, since the software relationships have been observed with respect to algorithms, and algorithms can be considered to be distillations of human thought, it follows that the abstracts of technical papers, which are in a similar sense distillations of the papers themselves, should provide a proper set of experimental data.

In some journals, however, there is a tendency for abstracts to be advertisements for the scientific papers they precede, rather than digests of their contents. Such abstracts violate the second consideration above. One journal that has successfully resisted this tendency for decades is that of the American Geophysical Union, so the data set will be taken from their journal.

The continuous series of twelve abstracts, starting on page 402 of *EOS Transactions of the American Geophysical Union* (Volume 57, Number 5, May, 1976) meets all of the specifications, and has been selected as the test set. The first, and shortest, of these abstracts will be used as an example to illustrate the counting process. It is reproduced

Table 13.2
Sample Technical Abstract [*from EOS Transactions*
American Geophysical Union, 57 (5), 402 (May 1976)]

A NEW SEISMIC REFRACTION METHOD
THAT MAPS THE TOPOGRAPHY OF OCEANIC CRUSTAL LAYERS

K. McCamy (Lamont-Doherty Geological Observatory of
Columbia University, Palisades, New York 10964)

Observations at one or more ocean bottom seismographs of
refracted arrivals from shots distributed over a region define
one or more observed delay-time surfaces. Those surfaces
can be described by undulations is the refracting layer. A
method for mapping these undulations, using a least squares
inversion technique combined with three-dimensional ray
tracing is developed. The result of this new inversion technique is a three-dimensional model of the oceanic crust.

Table 13.3
Operator Analysis of Sample Abstract of Table 13.2

j	Operator	$f_{1,j}$	j	Operator	$f_{1,j}$	j	Operator	$f_{1,j}$
1	¶	1	10	in	1	19	more	2
2	UC	4	11	is	2	20	over	1
3	.	4	12	of	3	21	this	1
4	,	1	13	or	2	22	with	1
5	-	3	14	can	1	23	least	1
6	a	4	15	for	1	24	these	1
7	at	1	16	one	2	25	those	1
8	be	1	17	the	3	26	three	1
9	by	1	18	from	1			

$$\eta_1 = 26, \qquad N_1 = \sum_{j=1}^{j=\eta_1} f_{1,j} = 45$$

NOTE. Operator "¶" indicates paragraph; operator "UC" counts usage of upper case or capitalization

Table 13.4
Operand Analysis of Sample Abstract of Table 13.2

j	Operand	$f_{2,j}$	j	Operand	$f_{2,j}$	j	Operand	$f_{2,j}$
1	new	1	13	method	1	25	developed	1
2	ray	1	14	region	1	26	inversion	2
3	time	1	15	result	1	27	reflected	1
4	crust	1	16	mapping	1	28	technique	2
5	delay	1	17	oceanic	1	29	refracting	1
6	layer	1	18	squares	1	30	dimensional	2
7	model	1	19	tracing	1	31	distributed	1
8	ocean	1	20	arrivals	1	32	undulations	2
9	shots	1	21	combined	1	33	observations	1
10	using	1	22	observed	1	34	seismographs	1
11	bottom	1	23	surfaces	2			
12	define	1	24	described	1			

$$\eta_2' = 34, \qquad N_2 = \sum_{j=1}^{j=\eta_2} f_{2,j} = 39$$

directly in Table 13.2, and the detailed analysis is shown in Tables 13.3 and 13.4.

From the analysis of this sample abstract, the observed length is 84, and the gross operator and operand counts are 26 and 34, respectively. For $k = 0.4$, this gives

$$\eta_1 = 0.4\eta_1' = 10.4$$

and

$$\eta_2 = 0.4\eta_2' = 13.6$$

$$\hat{N} = \eta_1 \log_2 \eta_1 + \eta_2 \log_2 \eta_2 = 86$$

$$N = N_1 + N_2 = 84$$

where the agreement between the observed and calculated lengths is within 3%. It is of interest to note that if this single set of observations had been used to determine experimentally a value of k, it would yield 0.392.

Using precisely the same counting procedure for the complete sample produces the raw data given in Table 13.5.

Table 13.5
Observed Software Parameters
for Technical Abstracts

Abstract	η_1'	η_2'	N_1	N_2
(1)	26	34	45	39
(2)	41	74	133	97
(3)	35	60	84	73
(4)	31	65	93	86
(5)	39	94	131	130
(6)	34	84	109	113
(7)	39	100	153	153
(8)	44	112	145	149
(9)	56	152	267	197
(10)	99	263	438	436
(11)	36	86	116	137
(12)	50	108	171	144

Table 13.6
Validation of Length Relation for Series
of Technical Abstracts ($\eta = 0.4\eta'$)

Abstract	η_1	η_2	N	$\hat{N}$
(1)	10.4	13.6	84	86
(2)	16.4	29.6	230	211
(3)	14.0	24.0	157	163
(4)	12.4	26.0	179	167
(5)	15.6	37.6	261	259
(6)	13.6	33.6	222	222
(7)	15.6	40.0	306	275
(8)	17.6	44.8	294	319
(9)	22.4	60.8	464	461
(10)	39.4	105.2	874	915
(11)	14.4	34.4	253	231
(12)	20.0	43.2	315	321
Sum			3639	3630
Mean			303	302
Coefficient of Correlation:			0.997	

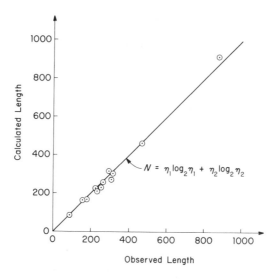

Figure 13.1   Length Relation Applied to Technical English

By multiplying the measurements of gross values of unique operators and operands in Table 13.5 by k, or 0.40, the values of η_1 and η_2 were obtained, as shown in Table 13.6. The standard length equation as derived in Chapter 2 then provided the values of $\hat{N}$.

While general conformity with the length relationship was to some extent expected before this experiment was undertaken, the precision of that agreement as demonstrated in Table 13.6 was almost incredible.

While it is certainly too early to attempt to assess the full significance of this experiment, it seems to indicate a more general applicability of the material of Chapter 2 than had originally been anticipated.

Just as the quantitative agreement of the length relationship for computer programs showed that rather fundamental elements were being measured and thereby encouraged the subsequent experiments, the same agreement here suggests that the parallelism be investigated further.

As a matter of conjecture, it is of some interest to calculate the potential volume, input/output parameters, implementation level, language level, elementary mental discriminations, and writing times for this set of technical abstracts. These properties have been calculated using the applicable equations from previous chapters, and the results are shown in Table 13.7. As a convenience, the equations are also repeated here in the order in which they are applied.

Passage level

$$L = \frac{2}{\eta_1} \frac{\eta_2}{N_2}$$

Volume

$$V = N \log_2 (\eta_1 + \eta_2)$$

Potential volume

$$V^* = L \times V$$

Potential operands η_2^*, obtained by solving, to the nearest integer value, from

$$V^* = (2 + \eta_2^*) \log_2 (2 + \eta_2^*)$$

Language level

$$\lambda = L^2 V$$

Effort

$$E = V/L$$

Time

$$T = E/S$$

where the Stroud number S is taken as 18 elementary discriminations per second.

At this point, we are tempted to consider the potential significance and intuitive consistency of each individual column of Table 13.7, but for most of them we must await the design of more objective methods of validation. Consider, for example, the potential volume or intelligence content V^*, or I, and the related parameter η_2^*. For computer programs, these values may be determined independently from a procedure call and then compared with the values resulting from analysis of the program itself. Further, two computer programs, even if written in different languages, can be taken as "saying the same thing" if they produce identical results when executed. Neither of these objective methods of validation appears applicable to English.

Nonetheless, one test is presently available which provides a tentative conclusion regarding the applicability to technical prose of the concept of potential volume.

Table 13.7
Software Properties of Technical Abstracts as Calculated
from Measurements of Table 13.5

Abstract	L	V	V^*	$\eta_2{}^*$	λ	E	T (minutes)
(1)	0.0671	385	26	6	1.73	5,740	5
(2)	0.0372	1270	47	11	1.76	34,100	32
(3)	0.4700	824	39	9	1.82	17,500	16
(4)	0.0488	955	47	11	2.27	19,600	18
(5)	0.0371	1496	55	12	2.06	40,400	37
(6)	0.0437	1234	54	12	2.36	28,200	26
(7)	0.0335	1774	59	13	1.99	59,900	49
(8)	0.0342	1753	60	13	2.05	51,300	48
(9)	0.0276	2960	82	17	2.25	107,000	99
(10)	0.0122	6272	77	16	0.94	512,000	474
(11)	0.0349	1419	49	11	1.73	40,700	38
(12)	0.0300	1884	57	13	1.70	62,800	58

This test is conducted in the following way. Using only the observed value of the length N, and the relationships of Chapter 4, we obtain estimates of η_1 and η_2, which may then be compared with their observed values. In principle, this procedure requires a value of λ, but because any prior knowledge of λ might invalidate the present experiment, we use only the roughest approximation and set $\lambda = 1$.

Because the results are too difficult to accept without them, each step of the procedure is given. First, the approximate relation

$$N = \eta \log_2 (\eta/2)$$

is used to obtain the value of η implied by N, and entered in Table 13.8 as $\eta (N)$. Second, N and $\eta(N)$ are used in the equation

$$V = N \log_2 \eta$$

to obtain the volume, entered as $V(N)$. Third, the equation

$$(V^*)^2 = \lambda V$$

with $\lambda = 1$, is used to obtain the potential volume from $V(N)$, and entered as $V^*(N)$. Fourth, the integer value of η_2^* is obtained from the relation

$$V^* = (2 + \eta_2^*) \log_2 (2 + \eta_2^*)$$

Table 13.8

Operator–Operand Distributions in Technical Abstracts: Theory vs Observation

Abstract	N	(N)	$V(N)$	$V^*(N)$	$\eta_2^*(N)$	$A(N)$	$B(N)$	$\eta_1(N)$	$\eta_2(N)$	η_1	η_2
(1)	84	24	385	19.62	5	0.944	3.11	11	13	10	14
(2)	230	50	1298	36.03	9	1.775	5.45	16	34	16	30
(3)	157	37	818	28.60	7	1.406	4.19	14	23	14	24
(4)	179	41	959	30.97	8	1.600	4.80	14	27	12	26
(5)	261	55	1509	38.85	9	1.775	5.45	18	37	16	38
(6)	222	48	1240	35.21	8	1.600	4.80	16	32	14	34
(7)	306	62	1822	42.68	10	1.935	6.13	19	43	16	40
(8)	294	60	1737	41.67	10	1.935	6.13	18	42	18	45
(9)	464	86	2982	54.61	12	2.216	7.57	24	62	22	61
(10)	874	142	6249	79.05	17	2.762	11.48	35	107	39	105
(11)	253	53	1449	38.07	9	1.775	5.45	17	36	14	34
(12)	315	63	1883	43.39	10	1.935	6.13	19	44	20	43
Sums								221	500	211	494
Means								18	42	18	41

using $V^*(N)$ and entered as $\eta_2^*(N)$. The relations

$$A = (\eta_2^* \log_2 (\eta_2^*/2))/(\eta_2^* + 2)$$

and

$$B = \eta_2^* - 2A$$

are then evaluated using $\eta_2^*(N)$. Finally, the unique operator and operand counts are calculated from

$$\eta_1 = (\eta - B)/(A + 1)$$

and

$$\eta_2 = A\eta_1 + B$$

and entered in Table 13.8 as $\eta_1(N)$ and $\eta_2(N)$, where they may be compared with the observations, rounded to the nearest integer, from Table 13.6.

In Table 13.8, the coefficient of correlation between $\eta_1(N)$ and η_1 is 0.977, and between $\eta_2(N)$ and η_2 it is 0.996.

It is difficult to see how this result could be explained if the concept of potential volume did not apply to this set of technical English abstracts.

Chapter 14

Application to Hardware

It has been demonstrated by Ostapko of IBM that the software relationships can be applied to hardware circuitry by expressing the circuitry as a computer program. With this approach, he was able to derive a relationship between the number of input–output pins of a package and the number of combinational circuits in the package.

This chapter outlines this derivation, and demonstrates its agreement with empirical evidence. Although based upon Ostapko's concepts, the derivation deviates considerably in detail by using the relationships of Chapter 4.

THE EMPIRICAL RELATION

Actual measurements of the number of circuits or gates versus the number of inputs and outputs for several early computers showed a certain regularity, which came to be called Rent's Rule, after E. F. Rent who first called attention to the phenomena in 1960. While some inconsistencies are found in the literature, we will base our evidence for the empirical relationship on the following two paragraphs, taken from Khambata's *Introduction to Large-Scale Integration* (Wiley, 1969). Khambata states (page 102):

> In designing any system it would be desirable to use some formula for the circuit-to-pin relationship as a guide. Such a formula, of necessity, would be an empirical relationship that would take into account the unique situation of the particular system and the actual experience associated with it. Such an empirical relationship, which has been satisfactory in most non-LSI cases, is

$$P_p = (FI_{av} + 1)(N_c)^{2/3} \qquad (1)$$

> where

P_p = the number of package logic pins (excluding pins for voltage supply and ground connections),

FI_{av} = average fan-in of logic circuits,

N_c = number of logic circuits in the package.

Equation 1 is basically applicable to IC's with a fairly low degree of logic functionality. From experience it is found that the average fan-in is 2.5 in many present systems. As the logic complexity of the package increases and the circuits are partitioned in a more optimized manner, (1) becomes less valid.

Khambata's expression of Rent's Rule, as quoted above, after substitution of his value of 2.5 for FI, is

$$P_p = 3.5N_c^{2/3} \qquad (14.1)$$

This formula is used to obtain representative empirical values of P_p for an appropriate range of circuits, for comparison with values to be derived from the hypothesis that follows.

THE SOFTWARE CIRCUIT HYPOTHESIS

The basic concept, which Ostapko presented, consists of identifying the number of pins P_p with the number of conceptually unique input/output parameters $\eta_2{}^*$ and the other elements of a logic package with their corresponding software properties.

First, we note that any 2-input, 1-output gate can be represented by the single statement

$$x_1 \text{ op } x_2 \rightarrow x_3 \; ;$$

where "op" represents the function of that gate, x_1 and x_2 are its input leads, and x_3 is its output. Consequently, it contains three operators (op $\rightarrow$;) and three operands ($x_1 x_2 x_3$).

As Ostpako pointed out, although combinational networks do not use circuits with a fan-in of 2 and a fan-out of 1, they could. A gate with FI inputs can be replaced by (FI − 1) gates with only two inputs each. By replacing the number of logic circuits in the package N_c by an equivalent number of 2-input, 1-output circuits $N_c{}'$ the analysis becomes fairly simple.

Most importantly, only two different gate types are required. With this condition, we have a maximum value for η_1 of only four for any possible package.

Because the total package can then be expressed with a single uniform statement for each of its $N_c{}'$ equivalent circuits, and since each statement will consist of three operators and three operands, its length N must be given by

$$N = 6N_c'$$

But from the length equation we also have

$$N = \eta_1 \log_2 \eta_1 + \eta_2 \log_2 \eta_2$$

where $\eta_1 = 4$ for all but the smallest packages. From Chapter 4, we have

$$\eta_2 = \eta_2{}^* + (\eta_1 - 2)\frac{\eta_2{}^* \log_2 (\eta_2{}^*/2)}{\eta_2{}^* + 2}$$

Consequently, with a knowledge of η_1, we may solve for η_2 for any value of $\eta_2{}^*$. Then, by solving for N, we may also obtain N_c'. Since

$$N_c' = (FI - 1)N_c$$

we may then use the value of FI = 2.5 cited earlier to obtain N_c as a single valued function of $\eta_2{}^*$ (or P_p).

As mentioned earlier, η must equal its maximum value of 4 for all but the smallest packages. For the extreme case of a package containing only

Table 14.1
Number of Circuits N_c as Function of Number of Pins
$\eta_2{}^*$—Theory vs Rent's Rule

$\eta_2{}^*$	η_2	N_c'	N_c	N_c (corr.)	N_c (Rent)
2	2	1.67	1.00	.78	0.43
3	3.70	2.50	1.67	01.38	0.79
4	5.33	3.48	2.32	2.10	1.22
5	6.89	4.53	3.02	2.86	1.71
6	8.38	5.61	3.74	3.64	2.24
8	11.20	7.84	5.23	5.19	3.46
10	13.87	10.10	6.74	6.72	4.83
15	20.13	15.86	10.58	10.58	8.87
20	26.04	21.74	14.50	14.50	13.66
30	37.33	33.82	22.55	22.55	25.09
50	58.93	59.09	39.40	39.40	53.99
100	111.07	127.12	84.75	84.75	152.72

one gate, however, η must be exactly 3. As a second gate is introduced, there is a 50% probability that η increases to 4, and so on.

Consequently, the minor error that is introduced at the lower end when the preceding equations are evaluated with $\eta_1 = 4$ may actually be corrected. Such a correction based on the value of N_c' as calculated both at $\eta_1 = 3$ and $\eta_1 = 4$, has been applied to N_c in Table 14.1, and shown as N_c (corrected). The values obtained may then be compared with empirical experience, as it is represented by equation (14.1), either in Table 14.1 or in figure 14.1.

Examination of figure 14.1 shows that as long as the number of pins is below 28, the difference between the theory and engineering experience is less than two circuits. Above that point, however, the software hypothesis predicts a smaller number of circuits than are actually used. This is compatible with the observation that in the larger networks, redundant circuits may be added in order to increase speed. If this is the case, they would constitute an impurity class, and as such would not be included in

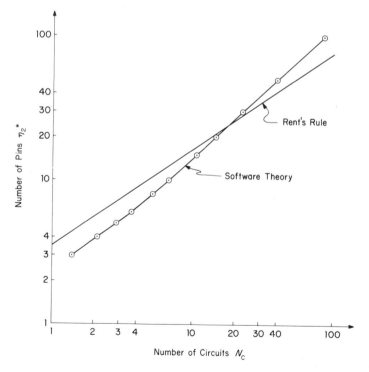

Figure 14.1   Circuits per Pin

the foregoing derivation. Studies have not yet been undertaken to determine whether or not this interpretation applies, but if it does, then the software hypothesis provides a lower limit for high values of pin number.

As Ostapko noted, the accuracy of estimating hardware requirements during the initial design phase is subject to improvement through better understanding of the dependence of the circuit requirements upon the independent parameter $\eta_2{}^*$.

Chapter 15

Application to Operating System Size

In a detailed study of the factors that contribute to the size of any given computer operating system, Elci noted a most interesting phenomena. By gathering and analyzing data on forty different operating systems, Elci found that the major part of the variation in the number of computer instructions required to control their resources depended only on the number of unique types or classes of resources involved. For his large sample, differences in design philosophy and in programming techniques were much less important in determining the size of the system than the simple scalar: number of unique types of resources controlled. Furthermore, Elci found that differences in the size contributions of different resource types were not statistically detectable. Elci's basic data are reproduced in Table 15.1. According to his definition, a resource type includes, for example, magnetic tape storage, but not the number of tape units. Similarly, his definition of operating system size is restricted to actual instructions, eliminating both tables and language compilers.

Elci demonstrated that the relations of software science can be employed to yield a reasonably accurate estimate of the number of resource types being managed by an operating system from the number of instructions in that system. In deriving the general relationship, we will largely, but not exclusively, follow the details and concepts of his treatment.

DERIVATION OF THE SYSTEM SIZE EQUATION

We denote the number of classes of allocatable resources by R_a, and the number of machine language instructions by P, corresponding to the last two columns of Table 15.1, respectively.

Only one basic assumption is required, to the effect that each unit increase in resources doubles the vocabulary, or

$$\eta = 2^{R_a} \tag{15.1}$$

Now in the approximate length equation (11.20), or

$$N = \eta \log_2 (\eta/2) \tag{15.2}$$

Table 15.1
Elci's Data on Number of Resources vs Number of Instructions
for 40 Operating Systems

	Operating System	Machine	Number of Resources	Number of Instructions
(1)	DUAL MACE	CDC 6500+6400	15	129,943
(2)	OS/MVT	IBM 360/65	14	84,894
(3)	OS/VSI	IBM 370/145	13	109,300
(4)	CP/67+CMS	IBM 360/67	13	64,363
(5)	EXEC 8	UNIVAC 1106	12	60,000
(6)	RSX 15	PDP 15/30	12	49,920
(7)	OS/MFT	IBM 370/155	12	48,094
(8)	OS/MVT	IBM 370/155	12	42,076
(9)	CTSS	IBM 7094	12	32,768
(10)	CTSS	IBM 7094	12	32,700
(11)	MAC SYSTEM	IBM 7094	12	32,000
(12)	GEORGE 3	ICL 1904A	11	40,000
(13)	PS/MFT	IBM 360/44	11	31,309
(14)	PS/MFT	IBM 360/40	11	29,632
(15)	CREOPS	NCR 4130	11	28,000
(16)	SAS	NCR 4130	11	21,000
(17)	SDC TSS	IBM AN/FSQ-32	11	16,384
(18)	MAXIMOP	ICL 1909	11	15,000
(19)	DOS 15	PDP 15/30	11	14,828
(20)	MINIMOP 2	ICL 1909	11	14,000
(21)	OS/1621	MICRODATA 1621	11	13,900
(22)	ZANEMAR	NCR 4130	11	12,000
(23)	V5	PDP 15/30	11	11,881
(24)	OS/MFT	IBM 370/145	10	21,312
(25)	M 3 0 S	MODCOMP III	10	8,058
(26)	M 2 0 S	MODCOMP II	10	8,058
(27)	R C 4000 MS	R C 4000	10	6,200
(28)	FOURIER OS	HP 2100S	10	6,042
(29)	TUMTR	IBM 7094	10	5,943
(30)	RT-11	PDP 11	10	5,250
(31)	ABMS	PDP 11	10	5,000
(32)	P C P	IBM 360/30	10	4,918
(33)	SNOS	DGC SUPERNOVA	10	4,801
(34)	DOS	IBM 360/30	10	3,219
(35)	SOS	DGC 800	9	2,816
(36)	SOS	DGC 800	9	2,816
(37)	DIG. FILTER	PSP 11/10	8	1,034
(38)	PILOT TSOS	UNIVAC 1108	7	474
(39)	TLMTR	IBM 7094	6	403
(40)	POLLY	μ PUP	5	16

we may substitute this assumption, obtaining

$$N = 2^{R_a} \log (2^{R_a - 1}) \tag{15.3}$$

or

$$N = (R_a - 1)2^{R_a} \tag{15.4}$$

Using the results of Knuth to estimate the average fraction of operands which are variables, and of variables which are indexed, as in equation (8.9) Chapter 8, we have

$$P = \frac{3}{8}N \tag{15.5}$$

from which we have the desired relationship

$$P = \frac{3}{8}(R_a - 1) \times 2^{R_a} \tag{15.6}$$

Table 15.2
Number of Resources per Operating System—
Theory vs Observation

System	R_a	$\hat{R}_a$	System	R_a	$\hat{R}_a$	System	R_a	$\hat{R}_a$
(1)	15	14.6	15	11	12.6	29	10	10.7
(2)	14	14.1	16	11	12.3	30	10	10.5
(3)	13	14.4	17	11	12.0	31	10	10.5
(4)	13	13.7	18	11	11.8	32	10	10.4
(5)	12	13.6	19	11	11.8	33	10	10.4
(6)	12	13.4	20	11	11.8	34	10	9.9
(7)	12	13.3	21	11	11.8	35	9	9.7
(8)	12	13.2	22	11	11.6	36	9	9.7
(9)	12	12.8	23	11	11.6	37	8	8.5
(10)	12	12.8	24	10	12.3	38	7	7.6
(11)	12	12.8	25	10	11.1	39	6	7.4
(12)	11	13.1	26	10	11.1	40	5	3.9
(13)	11	12.8	27	10	10.7			
(14)	11	12.7	28	10	10.7			

Sums			425	459.7	
Means			10.6	11.5	
Coefficient of correlation				0.954	

This relationship has the advantage of simplicity, in as much as the only arbitrary constant involved is the conversion factor from length to size, or 3/8.

COMPARISON OF SIZE HYPOTHESIS TO DATA

Entering equation (15.6) with the number of instructions in each of Elci's forty operating systems, one may obtain an estimate of its number of resources $\hat{R}_a$ as predicted by hypothesis. This value is then compared with the observed value R_a in Table 15.2.

Considering the simplicity of the derivation, and the complete absence of arbitrary constants, the fact that the relationship agrees as well as it does must lend support to Elci's hypothesis, as well as to his caution that adding "just one more" function to an operating system more than doubles its total size.

It should be noted, however, that the exceedingly large ranges in size corresponding to a given number of resources implies a similar lack of precision as an absolute forecasting technique, even though it does appear to provide a useful insight.

References

The first of the following two lists includes all of the Technical Reports, Doctoral Theses, and refereed journal articles that have contributed to the development of the material presented in this monograph. Items preceded by an asterisk contain experimental data.

The second list contains citations to that part of the general literature referenced in the discussions.

SOURCE REFERENCE LIST

1. Bayer, Rudolf. A Theoretical Study of Halstead's Software Phenomenon. Computer Science Department Technical Report 69, Purdue University. May 1972 (18 pages).
2. Bayer, Rudolf. On Program Volume and Program Modularization. Computer Science Department Technical Report 105, Purdue University. September 1973 (3 pages).
3.* Bell, D. E., and J. E. Sullivan. Further Investigations into the Complexity of Software. MITRE Technical Report 2874, Vol. II, June 30 1974.
4.* Bohrer, Robert. Halstead's Criterion and Statistical Algorithms. *Proceedings of the Eighth Annual Computer Science/Statistics Interface Symposium,* Los Angeles. February 1975, pp. 262–266.
5.* Bulut, Necdet. Invariant Properties of Algorithms. Ph.D. Thesis, Purdue University. August 1973 (215 pages).
6. Bulut, Necdet, and Maurice H. Halstead. Impurities Found in algorithm Implementations, Computer Science Department Technical Report 111, Purdue University. January 1974. [Also appeared in *ACM SIGPLAN Notices,* Vol. 9, no. 3, March 1974, pp. 9–10.]
7.* Bulut, Necdet, M. H. Halstead, and Rudolf Bayer. Experimental Validation of a Structural Property of Fortran Algorithms. Computer Science Department Technical Report 115, Purdue University. April 1974 (5 pages). [Also appeared in *Proceedings of the ACM Annual Conference.* San Diego. November 1974, pp. 207–211.]
8.* Elci, Atilla. Factors Effecting the Program Size of Control Functions of Fortran Programs. Ph.D. Thesis, Purdue University. December 1975 (134 pages).

9.* Elci, Atilla. The Dependence of Operating System Size upon Allocatable Resources. Computer Science Department Technical Report 175, Purdue University. December 1975 (20 pages).

10.* Elshoff, James L. Measuring Commercial PL/I Programs Using Halstead's Criteria, General Motors Research Publication, GMR–2012. November 1975. [Also appeared in *ACM SIGPLAN Notices* vol. 1, no. 5, pp. 38–46.]

11.* Funami, Yasuo, and M. H. Halstead. Software Physics Analysis of Akiyama's Debugging Data. Computer Science Department Technical Report 144, Purdue University. May 1975. [An expanded version appears in *Proc. MRI XXIV International Symposium: Software Engineering*. New York: Polytechnic Press, 1976.]

12.* Gordon, R. D., and M. H. Halstead. An Experiment Comparing Fortran Programming Times with the Software Physics Hypothesis. Computer Science Department Technical Report 167, Purdue University. October 1975. [Also appears in *AFIPS Conference Proceedings,* vol. 5, 1976 National Computer Conference (3 pages).]

13.* Halstead, M. H. A Thermodynamics of Algorithms. Computer Science Department Technical Report 66, Purdue University. February 1972 (8 pages).

14.* Halstead, M. H. Natural Laws Controlling Algorithm Structure?*ACM SIGPLAN Notices,* vol. 7, no. 2, February 1972, pp. 19–26.

15.* Halstead, M. H. A Theoretical Relationship between Mental Work and Machine Language Programming. Computer Science Department Technical Report 67, Purdue University. May 1972 (7 pages).

16.* Halstead, M. H., and Rudolf Bayer. Algorithm Dynamics. Computer Science Department Technical Report 72, Purdue University. May 1972. [Parts 1 and 2 of this 3 part report also appear in *Proceedings of ACM Annual Conference,* Atlanta, August 1973, pp. 126–135.]

17.* Halstead, M. H. An Experimental Determination of the "Purity" of a Trivial Algorithm. Computer Science Department Technical Report 73, Purdue University. September 1972. [Also appears in *ACM SIGME Performance Evaluation Review,* vol. 2, no. 1, March 1973, pp. 10–15.]

18. Halstead, M. H. Language Level, A Missing Concept in Information Theory. Computer Science Department Technical Report 75, Purdue University. September 1972. [Also appears in *ACM SIGME Performance Evaluation Review,* vol. 2, no. 1, March 1973, pp. 7–9.]

19. Halstead, M. H., and P. M. Zislis. Experimental Verification of Two Theorems of Software Physics. Computer Science Department Technical Report 97, Purdue University. June 1973 (11 pages).

20.* Halstead, M. H. Software Physics Comparison of a Sample Program in DSL ALPHA and Cobol. *IBM Research Report,* RJ1460. October 1974 (24 pages).

21.* Halstead, M. H. Software Physics: Basic Principles. *IBM Research Report,* RJ1582. May 1975 (64 pages).

22.* Halstead, M. H. Toward a Theoretical Basis for Estimating Programming Effort. Computer Science Department Technical Report 143, Purdue University. May 1975. [Also appears in *Proceedings ACM Annual Conference,* Minneapolis. October 1975, pp. 222–224.]

23.* Halstead, Maurice H., James L. Elshoff, and Ronald D. Gordon. On Software Physics and GM's PL/I Programs. General Motors Research Report, GMR–2175, June 1976 (26 pages).

24. Halstead, M. H. The Essential Design Criterion for Computer Languages. Panelist's Position Paper for Dr. Herbert Maisel's Session at National Computer Conference—1976. Technical Report 191, Computer Science Department, Purdue University. June 1976 (8 pages).

25. Halstead, M. H. Using the Methodology of Natural Science to Understand Software. Panelist's Position Paper for Dr. Roger Firestones Session at National Computer Conference—1976. Technical Report 190, Computer Science Department, Purdue University. June 1976 (7 pages).

26.* Harvill, J. B., and William C. Nylin, Jr. Multiple Tense Programming, A New Concept for Program Complexity Reduction. Technical Report CS75021, Southern Methodist University. December 1975.

27.* Ingojo, Jose C. Modularization in the Pilot Compiler and Its Effect on the Length. Computer Science Department Technical Report 169, Purdue University. November 1975 (35 pages).

28.* Kennedy, Dale, and Roger Bruning. Children's Descriptions of Complex Objects. Psychology Department Technical Report 505–68–6939, University of Nebraska. 1974 (4 pages).

29.* Kulm, Gerald. An Alternative Measure of Reading Complexity. Mathematics Department Technical Report, Purdue University, 1974. [Also presented at American Psychological Association Annual Meeting, New Orleans, August 1974 (14 pages).]

30.* Kulm, Gerald. Language Level and Information Content Measures in Mathematical English. Mathematics Department Report, Purdue University, 1974.

31.* Kulm, Gerald. Language Level Applied to the Information Content of Technical Prose. In *Collective Phenomena and the Applications of Physics to Other Fields of Science.* Prepared for delivery at a seminar, Moscow, USSR, 1–5, July 1974. (Norman A. Chigier and Edward A. Stern, eds.), Fayetteville, N.Y.: Brain Research Publications, 1975, pp. 401–408.

32.* Ostapko, Daniel L. On Deriving a Relation Between Circuits and Input/output by Analyzing an Equivalent Program. *ACM SIGPLAN Notices,* vol. 8, no. 6, June 1974, pp. 18–24.

33. Ottenstein, Karl J. A Program to Count Operators and Operands for ANSI–Fortran Modules. Technical Report 196, Computer Science Department, Purdue University. June 1976 (33 pages).

34.* Ottenstein, Karl J. An Algorithmic Approach to the Detection and Prevention of Plagiarism. Computer Science Department Technical Report 200, Purdue University. August 1976 (22 pages).

35. Ostapko, D. L. Analysis of Algorithms Implemented in Software and Hardware. *Proceedings of ACM Annual Conference,* San Diego, November 1974, p. 749.

36.* Zislis, Paul M. An Experiment in Algorithm Implementation. Computer Science Department Technical Report 96, Purdue University. June 1973 (253 pages).

37. Zislis, Paul M. Semantic Partitioning: An Aid to Program Testing. Ph.D. Thesis, Purdue University. June 1974.

38. Zislis, Paul M. Semantic Decomposition of Computer Programs: An Aid to Program Testing, *Acta Informatica,* vol. 4, 1975, pp. 245–269.

39. Zweben, Stuart H. Software Physics: Resolution of an Ambiguity in the Counting Procedure. Computer Science Department Technical Report 93, Purdue University. April 1973 (7 pages).

40.* Zweben, Stuart H. The Internal Structure of Algorithms. Ph.D. Thesis, Purdue University. May 1974 (171 pages).

41. Zweben, S. H. A Recent Approach to the Study of Algorithms. *Proceedings ACM Annual Conference,* San Diego, November 1974, pp. 747–748.

GENERAL REFERENCE LIST

Akiyama, F. An Example of Software System Debugging. *Proceedings, International Federation of Information Processing Societies (IFIPS) Congress, 1971.* Amsterdam: North-Holland, 1971, pp. 353–359.

Backus, John, *et al.* The Fortran Automatic Coding System. *Proceedings of the Western Joint Computer Conference (WJCC),* vol. 11, 1957, pp. 189–198.

Clausen, Robert. Euclidean Algorithm. *Communications of the Association for Computing Machinery, (CACM),* vol. 3, no. 4, April 1960, p. 240.

Garrett, George A. Management Problems of an Aerospace Computer Center. *Proceedings, Fall Joint Computer Conference (FJCC),* 1965, pp. 129–137.

Khambata, Adi J. *Introduction to Large-Scale Integration.* New York: Wiley, 1969.

Knuth, Donald E. An Empirical Study of Fortran Programs. *Software–Practice and Engineering,* vol. 1, no. 2, 1971.

Knuth, Donald. *The Art of Computer Programming,* vol. 1. Reading, MA: Addison-Wesley, 1969.

Liapunov, A. A. *Matematika v SSSR za Sorok Let 1917–1957.* Moscow, 1959, pp. 857–877.

MacKay, D. M. Quantal Aspects of Scientific Information. Proceedings, Symposium on Information Theory, London, September, 1950. [Also appears in *Transactions,* Institute of Radio Engineers, PGIT–1, February, 1953, pp. 60–80.]

Mandelbrot, B. Contribution a la Theorie Mathematique des Jeux de Communication. Ph.D. Thesis, University of Paris. December 1952. [Also appears in *l'Inst. de Statistique de l'Université de Paris,* vol. 2, 1953.]

Maurer, H. A., and M. R. Williams. *A Collection of Programming Problems and Techniques.* Englewood Cliffs, NJ: Prentice-Hall, 1972.

Miller, G. A., E. B. Newman, and E. A. Friedman. Length Frequency Statistics of Written English. *Information and Control,* vol. 1, 1958, pp. 370–389.

Shannon, C. E. A Mathematical Theory of Communication. *Bell System Technical Journal,* vol. 27, 1935, pp. 379–423.

Stroud, John M. The Fine Structure of Psychological Time. *Annals of New York Academy of Sciences,* 1966, pp. 623–631.

Zipf, G. K. *Human Behaviour and the Principle of Least Effort.* Reading, MA: Addison-Wesley, 1949.

INDEX

Numbers in italic type refer to figures in the text.

A. See Single valued functions of η_2^* (*A* and *B*).

Abstracts, technical, 98–110; operator-operand relation in, 109

Akiyama, F., 88

Ambiguous operands, 41

B. See Single valued functions of η_2^* (*A* and *B*).

Backus, John, 60

Basic metrics, 5–6

Bell, D. E., 84, 87–88, 95

Binary search, 46

Block size, 65

Bohrer, Robert, 12–13, 37, 65

Boundary volume, 21

Bugs, 85–91; initial, 84; delivered, 85

Bulut, Necdet, 65

Chunks, psychological, 85–88, 96

Circuitry, hardware, 111–115

Circuit-to-pin relation, 113

Common subexpressions, 9, 42

Compiler generated code, level of, 82

Complementary operations, 39

Concentration, mental, 48, 61

Content words as operands, 99

Control structures as operators, 8

Criteria for data selection: programs, 12; prose, 102

Debugging, 84–91

Difficulty. *See* Level.

E. See Effort (*E*).

Effort (*E*), 46–61; dimensions of, 48; equation, 47; as function of language level and parameter count, 82; mental, 47

Elci, Atilla, 116

Elshoff, James, 14, 65

English prose, 67, 98–110

Errors, 84–91; equation, 87; initial, 84

Euclid's algorithm, 7, 32, 36

Fan-in, 111

Fluency, requirement for, 61

Function words as operators, 99

Garrett, George, 70

Go-to statements: counting of, 7; effect on language level, 65

I. See Intelligence Content (*I*).

Impurities, 38–45; in circuits, 115; classes, 38; significance of, 45; removing from simultaneous equations, 74–76

Indexing instruction, 57

Information: content, 31; theory, 4, 31